WOMEN IN THE ACADEMY

For
Anne Baker

C. D. C. Reeve

WOMEN IN THE ACADEMY

Dialogues on
Themes from
Plato's *Republic*

Hackett Publishing Company, Inc.
Indianapolis/Cambridge

For further information, please address:

Hackett Publishing Company, Inc.
P.O. Box 44937
Indianapolis, IN 46244–0937

www.hackettpublishing.com

Cover design by Abigail Coyle

Library of Congress Cataloging-in-Publication Data

Reeve, C.D.C., 1948–
    Women in the academy : dialogues on themes from Plato's
Republic / C.D.C. Reeve.
        p.   cm.
    Includes bibliographical references.
    ISBN 0-87220-602-5 (cloth) — ISBN 0-87220-601-7 (paper)
    1. Women.   2. Plato. Republic.   I. Title.

HQ1206 R425 2001
305.4—dc21   2001026400

CONTENTS

PREFACE

A little over a decade ago, I read in Diogenes Laertius that among the students in Plato's school, the Academy, were two women, Axiothea of Phlius, "reported by Dicerarchus to have worn men's clothes,"[1] and Lasthenia of Mantinea. Who, I wondered, were these women? And what was it like for them to be in the Academy? On these questions, unfortunately, the historical evidence was silent. So I was forced to use my imagination. What emerged in the succeeding years was a series of five dialogues focusing on Plato's *Republic*, in which these women take part. Together they constitute an introduction to some of the central themes of that work. I think of them not just as aids to understanding, however, but as spurs to further thought. For the *Republic*, in my experience, is a dialogue that invites and inspires dialogue. Few come away from it silent.

Most of the dialogues were originally presented at Reed College to freshmen who had read (at breakneck speed!) Homer's *Iliad*, Hesiod's *Theogony* and *Works and Days*, Aeschylus' *Oresteia*, Herodotus' *Histories*, Sophocles' *Antigone* and *Oedipus Tyrannus*, Thucydides' *History of the Peloponnesian War*, Aristophanes' *Clouds*, and Plato's *Euthyphro*, *Apology*, and *Crito*. However, the dialogues themselves demand little knowledge of ancient Greece or of philosophy beyond what can be gleaned from the *Republic* itself.

The order in which they are printed traces out my own favored first path through the *Republic*: Books 2–4, 5 (to 471c), 10 (to 608b); 5 (471c–end), 6–7; 8–10 (608c–end); 1. But because each dialogue is more or less self-contained, readers should feel free to read them in whatever order makes the most sense to them.

---

1. Diogenes Laertius, *Lives of Eminent Philosophers* 3.46 (also 4.2). Diogenes probably lived in the first half of the third century A.D. Dicerarchus, who flourished c.300 B.C., was a student of Aristotle's. Of his many works only a few fragments survive. The Academy, located northwest of the Dipylon Gate in Athens, was founded in the mid-fourth century B.C.

The dialogue now called "Women" was first printed in a slightly different form by Hackett Publishing Company as part of its Fall 1992 Complete Catalogue. The piece was subsequently reprinted in *The Fortnightly Review* (Sri Lanka, 1994) and—again in a slightly different form—in Richard Kraut (ed.), *Plato's Republic: Critical Essays* (Lanham, Md., 1997). It appeared in Japanese in *Aichi* (Kobe, 1995). The other dialogues appear here for the first time.

"Freedom" has a history of a somewhat different sort. On one occasion, I presented it as a drama. I played the part of Plato, and Professor X—an untenured woman—played the part of Axiothea. Some of my colleagues considered this inappropriate. Students, they claimed, would confuse the relationship between the characters with the one between the actors and infer that I must dominate Professor X in real life in the way Plato dominates Axiothea (something he doesn't do, I think)! Some even suggested that to have a woman speak lines written by a man would offend against feminist principles. There could be no better proof, I think, of the contemporary pertinence of these dialogues, or of the topics with which they, and the *Republic*, deal: the nature of justice, freedom, and art, and the place of women in the Academy and the world.

I am very grateful to Jay Hullett for first publishing "Women" in its original, somewhat unusual format; to the many teachers who used it in their classes and urged me to produce some sequels; to Deborah Wilkes for encouraging me to respond to their urging; to my dear friend Paul Woodruff for his many helpful suggestions; and to the hundreds of Reed students who, over the course of almost a quarter of a century, have helped me understand the Greeks and the *Republic* better.

WOMEN

LASTHENIA: Women, Plato, I want to talk to you about women.

PLATO: I'm not sure I know much about them, to be honest.

LASTHENIA: Not women in general; women in the *Republic*.

PLATO: Oh, that's a different story. I have to say, though, that Socrates' views puzzle me almost as much as women themselves.

LASTHENIA: Well, maybe the two of us together will be able to solve some of those puzzles.

PLATO: Maybe so.

LASTHENIA: OK. I'll start with a bit of scene setting. In *Republic* 5, Glaucon and the others force Socrates to say more about the domestic lives of the guardians, the soldier-police of his ideal city, the kallipolis. He begins with the question of how female guardians should be trained and educated. Should they reduce the amount of work required of the males by sharing their duties, he asks, or be kept "at home as incapable of doing this, since they must bear and rear the puppies?" (451d). In other words, he wants to know whether these women should be active participants in the traditionally male world of honor, politics, and philosophy or be kept in seclusion because they're the ones who have babies. Socrates' opponent argues that because men and women have different reproductive roles, they must have different social roles, or do different jobs as well—which is what Socrates' own *principle of specialization* seems to prescribe. It's the one that requires each person in the kallipolis to stick exclusively to the single type of work for which his or her natural abilities are highest. Socrates fusses about that principle in *Republic* 2 and then uses it to define justice in *Republic* 4.

PLATO: I remember that.

LASTHENIA: You probably also remember, then, that Socrates sees through the opponent's argument: "In the case of both the male and the female sex, then, if one of them is shown to be different from the other with regard to a particular type of expertise or pursuit, we'll say that's the one that should be assigned to it. But if it's apparent that they differ in this respect alone—that the female bears the offspring, whereas the male mounts the female—we'll say it hasn't yet been proved that a woman's different from a man with regard to what we're talking about, and we'll continue to believe our guardians and their women should have the same pursuits" (454d–e). Hence, to defend his objection, the opponent must show that men and women have natural aptitudes for totally different things. And Socrates doesn't think he'll be able to do so. Why? Because on his view, though men are in general better than women at most things, "the various natural capacities are distributed in a similar way among both creatures, and women can share by nature in every pursuit, and men in every one" (455d–e). In other words, the general superiority of men to women provides no basis for assigning women as a sex to one set of tasks, and men as a sex to another. So women in the kallipolis aren't confined to the home but are trained for the job for which their natural aptitude's the highest—even though this means that people will have to get used to the sight of old women exercising naked in the gym alongside the men (452a–e). For, as Socrates rightly remarks, "It's foolish . . . to take seriously any standard of what's beautiful other than what's good" (452e).

All right. I understand that much. What I don't understand is whether these proposals are intended to apply to *all* women in the kallipolis or to only the *guardian* women. I don't think the text's very clear on this. So maybe you could tell me what you think Socrates had in mind.

PLATO: Well, the discussion of women, as I recall, is part of the account of the way of life of the guardians. As a result, female producers are never discussed in their own right. So it's easy to get the impression that Socrates' revolutionary proposals apply only to guardian women and that he intends female producers to lead lives modeled on those of their Athenian counterparts. But some stray remarks, which have clear application to female producers, suggest that the life envisaged for them may be quite different from that. In *Republic* 4, for example, Socrates remarks that the greatest cause of good to the kallipolis is the presence "in children and in *women*, in slaves and in free men, in producers, rulers, and subjects" of the principle that "each one should do his own work and not be meddlesome" (433d). The implication is that female producers—being just as subject to the principle of specialization as any other member of the kallipolis—will be trained in the one line of work for which they're naturally best suited. Since Socrates implies that there are women with natural aptitudes for carpentry (454d), explicitly mentions female physicians, and claims that natural aptitudes for each craft are to be found in both sexes (455d–e), he seems to intend female producers to be apprenticed in an appropriate trade in precisely the same way as the males. It could be, too, though again he isn't explicit on the matter, that he thinks *nursing* is a type of work to which the principle of specialization applies. If so, it will be put in the hands of those men and women who have a high natural aptitude for child care. Nonetheless, Socrates really is lamentably vague about the producers, whether male or female, and has simply left us somewhat in the dark on the important question of who will do the housework and rear the children, if, indeed, both parents are employed full-time in other jobs. Perhaps he should have provided day-care centers for older children in addition to the rearing pens he provides for infants.

LASTHENIA: That's interesting. Axiothea and I didn't pay enough attention to those passages when we were talking earlier.

PLATO: They're easy to overlook, and you aren't alone in failing to notice them. Others have done so as well, claiming that Socrates is a "feminist" only where guardian women are concerned.

LASTHENIA: I'm glad you brought up the issue of feminism, because that's the next topic I want to ask you about. Do you think Socrates really is a feminist? Does he have a special interest in the welfare of women?

PLATO: If a feminist is someone with a special interest in the welfare of women, is a "masculinist" someone with a special interest in the welfare of men?

LASTHENIA: I suppose so.

PLATO: Then Socrates is both a masculinist and a feminist, since he seems to be interested in the welfare of people generally, whether male or female. The impression I sometimes get, however, is that a feminist is someone who's *primarily*—maybe even exclusively—interested in the welfare of women. If so, then Socrates is neither a feminist nor a masculinist, and no one who cared about justice would be, either. Don't you agree?

LASTHENIA: Well, I see your point, anyway. You mean it's unjust to give more weight to the welfare of women than to that of people generally?

PLATO: Right.

LASTHENIA: You don't dispute, though, do you, that it's reasonable to devote more of one's energies to the welfare of those who are more oppressed?

PLATO: No, of course not. It's just that some feminists seem to think that men are simply a curse, whereas Socrates' view is that *bad* men are a curse and *bad* women, too. So he's neither like those men who retell the myth of Pandora, in which women are represented as the source of all evil, nor like those women who believe equally obnoxious myths about men.

LASTHENIA: Don't you think, though, that for all his revolutionary views about women, Socrates is really a male chauvinist at heart?

PLATO: How do you mean?

LASTHENIA: Consider the following passage and you'll see: "Now one finds all kinds of diverse desires, pleasures, and pains mostly in children, *women*, household slaves, and those of the inferior majority who are so-called free" (431b–c). Notice how Socrates groups women together with slaves, children, and the inferior majority. That doesn't sound very liberated. Here's a second example: "Don't you think it's slavish and money-loving to strip a corpse? And isn't it small-minded and *womanish* to regard a dead body as your enemy, when the enemy himself has flitted away, leaving behind only the instrument with which he fought? Do you think that people who do this are any different from the female dogs who get angry with the stones thrown at them but leave the person throwing them alone?" (469d–e). Just think how Axiothea and I feel when we hear him saying something like that. It's bad enough when guys in the gym say such things, but when our heroes and teachers say them, it's a lot worse.

PLATO: I'm sure it is. But I'm not persuaded that what Socrates says should upset you. You see, he's talking about women as they were in Athens in his day and as they still are—women who've been oppressed by men and kept in seclusion. He'd hardly say the same things about women in the kallipolis, or about liberally educated women in the Academy, like you and Axiothea. Or do you think he would?

LASTHENIA: I don't know, Plato. I honestly don't.

PLATO: Well, I can't believe he means to disparage women as such, but only women who've been turned into empty-headed creatures by an even emptier-headed society.

LASTHENIA: That defense may work for the cases I've cited so far, but will it work for this one, I wonder: "Do you know of anything practiced by human beings, then, at which *the male sex isn't superior to the female in all those ways*?" (455c). Here, Socrates seems to be talking about women *as such* and claiming that they're inferior to men at everything. But, in making that claim, it seems to me, he's illegitimately extrapolating from facts about *oppressed* women—for that's the only kind there have ever been!—to conclusions about women in general, including women who've been given the same opportunities as men.

PLATO: My goodness, I think you're right! Socrates does seem to have forgotten that the evidence for his claim is tainted, and that in the kallipolis, or any other just and nonoppressive society, the female sex might turn out to be far superior to the male at everything.

LASTHENIA: There's an even more damning piece of evidence, too. "The uttermost freedom for the majority is reached in a democratic city," Socrates claims, "when bought slaves, both male and female, are no less free than those who bought them. *And I almost forgot to mention the extent of the legal equality of men and women and of the freedom in the relations between them*" (563b). Doesn't Socrates imply here that legal equality between men and women is something bad, something he's not planning to incorporate into the kallipolis?

PLATO: He *seems* to imply this, I agree. But implications aren't explicit statements. And we have his explicit statements, in

Republic 5, that men and women with equal natural abilities *will* receive equal treatment in the kallipolis. In any case, it's surely possible that what Socrates is criticizing is the fact that democratic cities ignore natural abilities altogether and so treat people with *unequal* natural abilities as equals.

LASTHENIA: Well, I suppose the text could mean that. In any case, I agree that what Socrates says in *Republic* 5 is more important.

PLATO: Friends are important, too, Lasthenia. But the truth's much more important. You know as well as I do that Socrates himself would have wanted us to follow the argument wherever it led, even if it meant refuting him.

LASTHENIA: Wait a minute, Plato, you can't leave yet! You haven't heard my best argument!

PLATO: Oh? Let's hear it, then. I'm in no hurry.

LASTHENIA: If women and men were treated equally in the kallipolis, wouldn't the things women value have to be given as much initial weight as the things men do?

PLATO: I suppose so.

LASTHENIA: Well, men traditionally place a very high value on such things as warfare and philosophy, don't they?

PLATO: Yes.

LASTHENIA: Whereas women don't traditionally value these things at all?

PLATO: That's right.

LASTHENIA: They value weaving, cooking, bringing up children, and the emotional closeness and intimacy that married life makes possible. Anyway, that's what's traditionally been true of them.

PLATO: Yes.

LASTHENIA: Then, if men and women were treated equally in the kallipolis, these two lots of things—public life and domestic life, as I'll call them for short—would have to be assigned equal weight, at least, initially. But surely they aren't. Instead, Socrates just assumes that public life is valuable, that anyone, male or female, will want to engage in it if he can, and that domestic life, by contrast, is of very little value. As a result, he forbids the male and female guardians to live together as man and wife in private houses and puts the rearing of children—anyway, guardian children—in the hands of nurses. In other words, he deprives the guardians of intimacy and domestic life altogether.

The result, it seems to me, is that Socrates hasn't treated women justly at all and hasn't shown the same interest in their welfare as in that of men. What he *has* done is made an entirely masculinized world and then given women the freedom to be "men" in it. That isn't equal treatment.

You can see this clearly if you imagine the kind of kallipolis a woman might have designed, where men were given the freedom to weave, cook, and bring up children but found that philosophy and fighting had been excluded altogether or put exclusively into the hands of others. What *man*, looking at such a society, would think that men were treated with equal justice there? So the hegemony of males in the kallipolis is more subtle and insidious than it first seems. In fact, it has so infected the imagination of Socrates that his kallipolis is tainted with it in a way that even he doesn't seem to notice.

The result, though, is that his ideal society—while it strives to treat men and women equally—actually subordinates women to men more effectively than ever, by excluding women's values almost entirely. What it gives us isn't a world in which men and women are treated equally, but a world in which *women* don't exist, a world that is really a world of men with penises and men without them.

Closer to home, you've no doubt noticed that Axiothea wears men's clothes here in the Academy. This shows, I think, what a masculinized place it is, for all that you're open-minded enough to admit women students to it.

PLATO: Whew, Lasthenia, I haven't heard *that* before! What a good thing you *are* here! No man, not even one as bright as Aristotle,[1] could have come up with that criticism. It's such a good one, in fact, and raises so many doubts in my mind about my own imagination, and how *it* may have been colored by the insidious sexism

---

1. Aristotle (384–322 B.C.), the great philosopher from Stagira, joined the Academy at the age of seventeen and remained there until the death of Plato in 348/7 B.C. He appears in the dialogue "Forms."

you mention, that I'm almost afraid to criticize it. I'm afraid, frankly, of seeming to be just another male oppressor of women. So let me ask you this: Are you willing to let the argument decide between us? Or will I lose your respect or become your enemy if I argue with you?

LASTHENIA: A few days ago, I told Axiothea that argument and dialectic—what we do here in the Academy under the name of philosophy—is aggression and competition with words instead of swords. One of the other students—I think it was Aristotle, as a matter of fact—overheard me. He said, "the rational part of the soul has no gender." He meant that reason—and hence philosophy, argument, and dialectic—is neither male nor female.

I didn't quite know what to say to that. But afterward Axiothea put the issue to me somewhat differently. She said it would be foolish for women to treat anything that might do them some good as masculinized and unusable. Women should be opportunists, not purists, willing to use pretty well anything to liberate themselves.

I think she's right about that. Women weaken themselves when they reject what men have made as too impure for them to use. We should take the good, no matter who has made it, and get rid of the bad, even if it's something that women have long held dear—like marriage, for example. So I suppose I'm willing to hear what you have to say. But if I think the conclusion will help oppress women or make them accept oppression, I won't agree to it. For no truly objective and unbiased philosophical argument could support a conclusion like that.

PLATO: Axiothea's advice was good, I think, and your provisos are no doubt wise. What I have to offer in response is a fable I once heard, not from a man, but from Diotima, a wise woman from your own city of Mantinea. She said that when the gods were making the world, they gave good things to all the animals, and also things that seemed good but weren't. Among the things they gave to human beings were those you mentioned earlier: philosophy, warfare, weaving, cooking, and the capacity to form deep emotional ties, live in households, and rear offspring successfully. They gave these things to human beings in a more or less random fashion. But because of the luck of the draw, men mostly got what fitted them for public life and women mostly got what fitted them for domestic life. As time went by, and habit and tradition did their work, each sex came to see the things it had been given as the real goods, and those given to the other sex as merely apparent goods. That was what Diotima told me. And what she meant, I imagine, is that we can't settle on which of these things are really good just by appealing to what their possessors think. For each sex sees what it got, as opposed to what the other sex got, as really good. And they both can't be right about that!

LASTHENIA: I think I see what you mean. If the things men traditionally value are the really good things, while those women traditionally value are only apparently good, Socrates won't have been unjust to women in doing what I described as masculinizing the kallipolis. For the goods women are deprived of will be apparent goods, while those they're given will be real ones. It was clever of Diotima to have noticed that objection to my argument. And I thought that *I* was the first woman philosopher from Mantinea! But is it really a compelling objection? Is it really plausible to believe that all women are wrong in finding value in their traditional activities and pursuits and that all men are right in finding value in theirs?

PLATO: I can best answer you, I think, with another of Diotima's stories. In this one, the gods gave everyone all the true and apparent goods and everyone agreed that the ones appropriate to domestic life were the really valuable ones. So, because the men were physically stronger, they tried to take these for themselves, leaving warfare and philosophy to the women. But the men couldn't bear or suckle children. So they were forced to give them to the women for the first five years. Well, the women fed their sons' heads with tales of military valor and the joys of philosophy and portrayed their fathers as sissies. In due course, when habit and tradition had done their work, all the men were devoted to warfare and philosophy and the women had all the really good things to themselves.

LASTHENIA: Oh, I get it now! The point is that opinions about what's valuable can't settle the question of what's really valuable, because those opinions are socially formed. And that's true whether they're men's opinions or women's. But if that's right— if we can't appeal to the testimony of people about what is and isn't valuable—then how are we to determine whether Socrates has been unjust to women in masculinizing the kallipolis, or has simply given them true goods in place of apparent ones?

PLATO: It seems to me that that's really what the *Republic*'s about.

LASTHENIA: Right, right! I'd almost forgotten that the *Republic* isn't primarily about women, but about how we might acquire stable and objective knowledge of values and use it to construct a just society. But, Plato, we don't have that knowledge, and maybe we'll never have it. So what are we to do in the meantime?

PLATO: In the meantime, we should recognize that we don't have the kind of knowledge of values that would justify us in being dogmatic about them and that we should strain every nerve to acquire it. For, when you come to think about it, it just isn't obvious, is it, whether either the lives of warriors or those of homemakers are really the best ones?

LASTHENIA: What about the philosophical life, Plato? Is the same true of it? Might philosophy turn out to be something that we simply have to give up?

PLATO: That's hard to answer in the abstract. Nonetheless, it was philosophy that enabled Socrates to see through so many of the bad arguments men have used to justify their oppression of women. It was philosophy, too, that enabled him to overcome his own culture's prejudices as far as he did. Maybe he didn't see everything we think he ought to have seen. Maybe he made some mistakes. But isn't it your own knowledge of philosophy, isn't it your own training here in the Academy that has enabled you to diagnose his errors and do better?

LASTHENIA: I worry still, though, that philosophy is so competitive, so much like fighting, so—if you'll forgive me—male.

PLATO: Philosophy wears men's clothes, Lasthenia, because it has been the prerogative of males.

LASTHENIA: But underneath the clothes it's neither male nor female—is that what you're saying?

PLATO: Aristotle said that reason has no gender. I think the same might be said of philosophy.

LASTHENIA: I wonder whether you'd still think that, Plato, if you had to wear *women's* clothes in order to feel comfortable practicing it.

Plato was called away before he could respond. A few days later, I wrote down what I could remember of our conversation. It seemed to me, in that quiet hour, that my own objections to Socrates were too abstract, too "philosophical." Other, more concrete ones—drawn from experience, not philosophy—crowded into my mind. For example, Socrates says that the best women will be assigned as frequent sex partners to the best men by a rigged lottery (458c–460b). What would happen, though, to women like Axiothea, who don't want to have sex with men?

Moreover, since the best women have sex more often, they will be more often pregnant—far more often than their inferior sisters. But frequent pregnancy is debilitating and often life-threatening. Everyone knows that. So their chances of becoming philosopher-kings at the age of fifty-five are likely to be quite low—substantially lower than those of a comparable male guardian. Hence women, just because they bear children, are less well off in the kallipolis than men with the same natural abilities.

I don't claim that there are no answers to these difficulties. In fact, Axiothea pointed out to me that pregnant women could stay at home reading philosophy and getting ready for their exams, while the men risked their lives on the battlefield or performed other onerous duties. But the point remains that Socrates doesn't even notice these problems. And that shows, I think, that he hasn't thought carefully enough about the women of the kallipolis or the lives they will lead there.

In the months that followed, I reflected further on these topics. I found myself wondering whether anything could be done to prevent the biological differences between men and women from resulting in social differences prejudicial to women. I thought about how sex and reproduction might be separated, about genderless societies, about same-sex couples, and about how the burdens (and joys) of childbearing and child rearing might be better shared between men and women. Soon I hope to write a *Republic* of my own.

ART

AXIOTHEA: I'm sure *I* could get in. When they think you're a man, they let you go anywhere! I went to a symposium a few weeks ago—lovely flute girls!—and no one paid the least attention.

LASTHENIA: What about your voice—didn't it give you away? And your breasts . . .

AXIOTHEA: I told them in a hoarse voice that I had a cold and needed to keep my cloak on. That was enough to cover me on both fronts! Men aren't very observant, especially when there are pretty girls to ogle and wine to drink.

LASTHENIA: Still, the theater . . . they'd be sure to catch you.[1] And I just don't have the courage to dress like a man . . . or the skill to pass as one.

AXIOTHEA: Oh, all right! I won't go, either. I'll tell you what. Let's find Plato and ask him about his views on the theater. That should be good for a laugh!

LASTHENIA: Really, Axiothea, you should be serious about philosophy! It's no laughing matter, certainly not to Plato. If he thought we were laughing at him . . .

AXIOTHEA: He'd join in! He's serious, not solemn. It isn't easy to tell what his own views are. He sees so many sides of an issue, he probably doesn't know himself!

---

1. Women did not take part in *symposia* (drinking parties) except as entertainers. The question of whether they could attend the theater is more difficult. Many believe—as I have assumed—that they could not. But Plato, *Gorgias* 502b–e and *Laws* 658a–d, 817a–c suggest that this assumption may be mistaken. See K. J. Dover, *Aristophanic Comedy* (Berkeley: University of California Press, 1972), 16–17; Roger Just, *Women in Athenian Law and Life* (London: Routledge, 1989), 109–10.

LASTHENIA: I know. I went to talk to him a while ago about the views he expresses about women in the *Republic*. He wouldn't even acknowledge they were his. He said that Socrates' views on women puzzled him almost as much as women themselves. As if we didn't know that Socrates is just his mouthpiece.

AXIOTHEA: Do we really know that? I think Plato's one of those people who's more comfortable and more creative when he's playing someone else's role.

LASTHENIA: Like you, you mean, pretending to be a man!

AXIOTHEA: Oh, there's always pretense involved *there*, even for a male! It's all theater, really. Plato's like a playwright; he divides himself up into many parts. Have you noticed what a superb mimic he is of other people's styles? You'd swear that speech in *Phaedrus* was actually by Lysias.[2]

LASTHENIA: I thought it was!

AXIOTHEA: Stop it! You'll be telling me next that you think the *Republic* reports a real conversation. It's all theater!

LASTHENIA: Look, there's Plato now. Let's catch up with him and see if he'll talk to us.

AXIOTHEA: Come on, then.

LASTHENIA: Plato! Hold on.

AXIOTHEA: What's that book you're reading?

PLATO: A big evil, Axiothea, as the saying goes. Books . . . I don't know. You can't question them. It isn't like having another person in front of you. They're full of ambiguities.

LASTHENIA: I suppose plays are the same in that respect, even though there you do have people in front of you.

PLATO: But they're playing roles, not expressing their own thoughts. You don't have to know how to run an army to play the part of a general.

---

2. *Phaedrus* 230e–234c. Lysias (459/8–c.380 B.C.) was a well-known Attic orator. The *Republic* is set at the house of his father, Cephalus.

AXIOTHEA: What about the playwright? Is Euripides[3] expressing his own thoughts when he writes a general's lines?

PLATO: Socrates used to say that poets are divinely inspired.[4] He was probably right. It's probably the gods who speak through them.

AXIOTHEA: Even in the case of Aristophanes?[5]

LASTHENIA: Oh, surely the gods can't inspire those filthy comedies!

AXIOTHEA: Why not? Zeus is hardly a paragon of virtue, and he's the god-in-chief![6]

LASTHENIA: Well, I don't believe the gods would inspire anyone to have Socrates burned to death, the way he is in *Clouds*.

PLATO: I agree with you, Lasthenia. The gods inspire us only to do good things.

AXIOTHEA: Odd, then, that they inspire even the tragic poets, like Homer, to represent gods as pretty bad![7]

PLATO: Excellent point! Clearly, the poets are divinely inspired only when they're speaking the truth. That's why it takes a philosopher—someone who knows the truth and loves it above all else—to edit the works of the poets, so that they become safe for ordinary people to read.

LASTHENIA: Socrates defends that sort of view in the *Republic*, doesn't he?

AXIOTHEA: Yes. He wants to banish poets from the kallipolis. Yet, I hear that he attended *Clouds* and stood up to be recognized when the actor who played him appeared on stage. If he was so critical of poets, why did he bother with their works?

---

3. Euripides (480s–407/6 B.C.) was an Athenian tragic playwright, sometimes alleged to have been influenced by Socrates.

4. Plato, *Ion* 533c–536d, *Phaedrus* 245a, *Laws* 719c.

5. Aristophanes (c.450–c.386 B.C.) was an Athenian comic playwright. His *Clouds*, mentioned by Lasthenia below, was produced in 423 B.C.

6. See *Republic* 377b–383c, 390b–c.

7. Homer (second half of the eighth century B.C.), author of the *Iliad* and *Odyssey*.

PLATO: "Know thy enemy," perhaps?

AXIOTHEA: "Love thy enemy," I think. It's like those people who pretend to study pornographic vase paintings because they admire the artist's style![8] Old Socrates probably laughed his head off along with everyone else and enjoyed being the center of things. I'll bet he had a whale of a time!

LASTHENIA: I don't think he was laughing when the people made him drink the hemlock, because they shared Aristophanes' views of him.[9] And I wish you wouldn't call him "old Socrates." That's an irreverent way to speak about him, especially when you're standing so close to his shrine.[10]

PLATO: I don't know how much laughing *anyone* did at *Clouds*. I was just five when it was first staged, but I remember hearing later that it was awarded only third prize. Socrates had a good sense of humor, though, I'll say that for him. He liked a bit of irreverence! When we were boys, following him around, we used to have trouble controlling ourselves. He'd be about to puncture some old windbag's ego by catching him in a contradiction, and we'd be so overcome when we saw the trap about to close that we'd have to pinch ourselves hard to stop from laughing out loud.

AXIOTHEA: Yes, some of your dialogues have that same effect on people still. They're almost as good as comedies, in that regard. In fact, they *are* a sort of theater, aren't they—plays with a thinking man as hero?

LASTHENIA: Really, Axiothea! Don't pay any attention to her, Plato, she's teasing you.

PLATO: No, no, philosophy may well be a sort of tragedy—the truest sort.[11]

---

8. Attic red-figure pottery includes many explicit images of various sorts of sexual activity. A good sample can be found in Eva C. Keuls, *The Reign of the Phallus* (Berkeley: University of California Press, 1993).

9. See Plato, *Apology* 18a–e.

10. I imagine, as seems likely, that there was a shrine or altar dedicated to Socrates within the precincts of the Academy or close by.

11. See Plato, *Laws* 817b.

AXIOTHEA: But whether they're comedies or tragedies, wouldn't they be banished from the kallipolis in either case?

LASTHENIA: No, of course they wouldn't. You see, Socrates never does banish the poets. He just requires them to work, like everyone else, under the guidance of philosophers, who can censor their works appropriately. So Plato's dialogues wouldn't be banned in the kallipolis, because they're actually written by a philosopher.

AXIOTHEA: Clever! But I'm not convinced. I mean, think about the principles that lie behind Socrates' censorship of poetry. The guardians should hear only the kinds of poetry that will help make them moderate and courageous, because moderation and courage are virtues a good guardian must have. Who'd want cowardly and avaricious soldier-police guarding them? By parity of reasoning, then, the producers in the kallipolis—the potters, shoemakers, builders, doctors, and so on—should hear only the sorts of poems that will inspire them with the traits good producers need. No point in having *them* be courageous and warlike! They should be peace-loving, industrious, frugal, and . . . well, you get the picture. So, now, here's my point. Plato's dialogues wouldn't be suitable for either producers or guardians. After all, they have a philosopher as hero, a master dialectician. But dialectic, if I remember correctly, is forbidden to everyone in the kallipolis except the philosophers. Presumably, then, if the dialogues are suitable for anyone, it will be for them. The trouble is, I can't see what use they'd be to people who are fully trained philosophers already. I mean, what would *they* have to gain from watching old Socrates—I'm sorry, from watching Socrates—refute the likes of Euthyphro?[12]

LASTHENIA: I don't recall Socrates making those points explicitly. My impression was that, just as in Athens, there'd be one theater and one poetry for everyone.

PLATO: That was my impression, too. But now that I hear what Axiothea has to say about how Socrates justifies his censorship of poetry, I'm inclined to think she's on to something. Since different

---

12. Euthyphro, Socrates' antagonist in the Platonic dialogue named after him, a self-proclaimed authority on Greek religion (4e4–5a2), manifests no great ability in philosophical argument.

social roles do seem to need to be supported by different kinds of poetry, Socrates should have provided one kind of poetry for the guardians and another for the producers. In the case of the philosophers, it's a bit more complex, since they come from the ranks of the guardians. . . .

AXIOTHEA: Right. So they should have the same poetry as the guardians, at least until such time as they're chosen as philosopher-kings. Then, they should have poetry of their own. I mean, they're hardly going to find stories about warriors all that inspiring when their own fighting days are over! But, again, these stories can hardly be your dialogues, since they'll be—forgive me for saying so—just too simpleminded, too elementary, for people who know so much philosophy already.

LASTHENIA: Wait a minute! I think I see where your mistake is. You think only philosopher-kings could legitimately read the dialogues or watch them being performed. But what about the apprenticed philosophers, the ones who aren't yet fully trained? After they've studied the mathematical sciences for ten years, they study dialectic for five (536d–540a). Well, what do you think they're studying, if not Plato's dialogues? Maybe, these dialogues *would* be too elementary for the full-blown philosopher-kings themselves, but, if our own experience is anything to go by, they'd be just the things that students of philosophy need to work through.

AXIOTHEA: How could I have overlooked something that's so much in front of my eyes! But is that really what *you* had in mind, Plato? Will the philosophy students in the kallipolis be studying the *Republic*?

PLATO: Well, having heard you both, I think that must be what Socrates intended—or, rather, what he would have said if he'd had you to question him instead of my poor brothers!

LASTHENIA: So you're wrong to say the dialogues are a type of theater, Axiothea. I mean, plays are play—forms of amusement, sources of pleasure—whereas your dialogues are schoolbooks, serious things, not play.

AXIOTHEA: That's too simpleminded! Remember when Socrates says children shouldn't be *forced* to learn mathematics? "Use play instead," he says (536e). And earlier he rightly castigates those who dismiss training in music and gymnastics as mere play (424d). 'Playful' is the opposite of 'solemn', not of 'serious'! I feel that we're at play here all the time. What could be more fun than working out geometrical proofs or having a good philosophical argument? We don't do it because we *have* to, we do it because we *enjoy* it. And I'll bet the same is true of the philosophers in the kallipolis.

PLATO: In fact, that *has* to be true of them. They must love argument for its own sake, but rule only to avoid being ruled by people worse than themselves (347a–e, 520a–521b).

LASTHENIA: I don't know. You two are obviously a lot more comfortable with the competitive side of argument than I am. I've never found Socrates all that amusing. I think he's cruel to people and enjoys crushing their egos and making them look stupid. There's a kind of arrogance in him that I find repellent. Besides, I really *like* reading Homer and Aeschylus and Sophocles, and I don't think I'll outgrow them by becoming a better or more knowledgeable philosopher.[13] In some ways, I think they're a lot wiser than Socrates. They know more about us and our lives. I don't think they'd be improved by being Socratized. I think they'd be ruined.

AXIOTHEA: Wait until you actually see them performed in the Theater of Dionysus![14]

PLATO: In the kallipolis, she'd be able to!

LASTHENIA: No, that's just it. I wouldn't. I'd be able to see watered-down, Socratized versions of them at best.

PLATO: Well, let's see. You say, Lasthenia, that you don't think you'll outgrow Sophocles by becoming a more mature philosopher. Maybe that's right. Maybe some parts of us rarely become

---

13. Aeschylus (525/4–456/5 B.C.), the Athenian tragic playwright, was the author of the *Oresteia*. Sophocles (496/5–406 B.C.), another great Athenian tragic playwright, was the author of *Antigone* and *Oedipus Tyrannus*.

14. Dionysus, son of Zeus and Semele, the daughter of Cadmus, was the god of wine, intoxication, and ecstasy. The theater was on the south slope of the Athenian Acropolis.

fully mature—I mean our appetites and emotions. If so, they'll continue to seek the satisfactions the theater brings, even if the rational, philosophical part of our soul has left them far behind.

AXIOTHEA: Well, then, they're going to be pretty frustrated in the kallipolis, where all they'll get is Socrocles!

LASTHENIA: Right! Remember Socrates censors *all* the poets in the kallipolis.

PLATO: All those that need it, certainly. But he also says, if I'm not mistaken, that "with a few rare exceptions," poetry is able to corrupt even good people (605c). I've always assumed that the philosophers—who are themselves somewhat rare birds (503d)—will be among those few. They can read or watch anything they like, because their appetites and emotions are in harmony with their reason. Wouldn't that have to be true, in fact, if they're going to act as censors of the poets? Moreover, it's clear that Socrates would be glad if poetry could be defended against his criticisms and readmitted to his city (607c–608b).

LASTHENIA: Before we go off on that topic, I think I see a way to make *my* worry a bit more precise. Suppose I'm right about the way Socrates comes across in the dialogues. How could it be appropriate, then, for the trainee philosophers in the kallipolis to learn dialectic by emulating him? They're supposed to "imitate someone who's willing to engage in discussion in order to look for the truth, rather than someone who plays at contradiction for sport" (539c). But Socrates, as I see him, often seems just as interested in the cruel sport of deflating egos as in the patient search for truth.

AXIOTHEA: And I think I know why. The patient search for truth makes for bad theater! Socrates says so himself: "But a rational and quiet character, which always remains pretty much the same, is neither easy to imitate nor easy to understand when imitated, especially not by a crowd consisting of all sorts of people gathered at a theater festival, for the experience being imitated is alien to them" (604e). I'm quoting from memory, so I may not have gotten it exactly right. But that's the gist anyway. I'm not sure about "all sorts of people gathered at a theater festival," but lots of ordinary people love to read or watch your dialogues, because they're mesmerized by Socrates. And that wouldn't be true, would it, if he had the character his philosophers possess? I mean it's obvious that what people like to see is Socrates wearing that old cloak of his, talking about his divine sign, making his strange grimaces, protesting his ignorance, and trying to look innocent while he's getting ready to deliver the killing blow. Would all those handsome young men have followed him around if he'd been just a colorless old man relying on the charms of logic alone?[15] I told you it was all theater, and now you can see how right I am!

LASTHENIA: You know, there's something in what Axiothea's saying, Plato. Socrates himself says that when poems have been "stripped of their musical colorings," they "resemble the faces of young men that aren't beautiful after the bloom of youth has left them" (601a–b). But mightn't one say the same about your own dialogues: if we took Socrates, with all his little personal foibles and eccentricities, out of them, wouldn't *they* be a lot less beautiful, too?

AXIOTHEA: Right. If the dramatic side of the dialogues isn't important, why not just give us the philosophy straight, the way Eudoxus gives us a geometrical proof?[16]

PLATO: Strange. I heard him talking yesterday about a "tragedy" that occurred in one of his classes when one of his favorite conjectures was refuted by your own counterexample! No doubt it was the tragedy of a theorem killed by a fact!

AXIOTHEA: You see, Lasthenia, I told you Plato could be funny!

LASTHENIA: Not as funny as we're being, going around in circles. I mean, if the dialogues are intended for philosophy *students*, maybe their dramatic elements are intended to make them more palatable to people who aren't quite ready for pure, unadulterated logic and philosophy. You know, we start out ourselves with dialogues, like *Euthyphro* and *Crito*, that are more dramatic and

15. See *Apology* 23c–d.
16. Eudoxus of Cnidus (c.390–c.340 B.C.) was an outstanding mathematician, who did important work in astronomy and geography and was also educated in medicine and philosophy. He was acquainted with Plato, certainly. It is less clear that he was actually a member of the Academy, though he is often confidently assumed to have been one. See W. K. C. Guthrie, *A History of Greek Philosophy*, Vol. V (Cambridge: Cambridge University Press, 1978), 446–57.

philosophically less challenging. Later on, when we're more experienced, we read *Parmenides* and *Sophist*. No one's ever suggested that they're an easy read! They're almost as devoid of dramatic color as those theorems you like so much.

AXIOTHEA: I see what you mean about going around in circles. But I wonder if Plato agrees with your explanation.

PLATO: You both know Theaetetus.[17] He was a brilliant mathematician, even as a young boy. You often see that in music, too; young children who are already proficient players. When it comes to the wisdom Socrates prized, though, you don't find it in young people.

AXIOTHEA: That's true, I suppose, but I don't see how it's relevant.

LASTHENIA: That's because you're young and mathematically gifted yourself! When you're as old as I am, you'll see right away what Plato means.

AXIOTHEA: Well, am I going to have to wait—what is it, four whole years!—or are you going to give me the benefit of your hard-won experience?

LASTHENIA: It takes emotional maturity to understand about virtue and vice and how to live. But in mathematics all you need is intelligence of the right sort. Four years can make a lot of difference.

AXIOTHEA: Oh, oh! I know what's coming, another of your little sermons about my dissolute life!

LASTHENIA: No, they don't do any good. You'll just have to learn that lesson the hard way, through suffering. But in the meantime, useless though it may be, I'll tell you what I'm getting at, and how it's relevant to our topic.

AXIOTHEA: Gee, thanks!

LASTHENIA: Suppose you're an honor-lover, so that the pleasure of getting the better of others is your sweetest pleasure. Well, that doesn't mean that you can't be a really good mathematician. You

---

17. Theaetetus of Athens (c.415–369 B.C.) was a significant geometer who focused on the theory of irrational lines. He figures in the Platonic dialogue that bears his name.

may work hard at your theorems because you want the honor you'll get from proving them, but that's no obstacle to your getting them right. If you don't get them right, indeed, you won't get the honor, either! And the reason it's no obstacle is that the theorems themselves have nothing to do with pleasure. I mean, Pythagoras' theorem about right triangles won't look wrong to you just because honor and approval are what your life's all about. In ethics, however, it's a different story. Suppose I have an argument, like the one in *Republic* 9, that the pleasure of knowing the truth is the sweetest, and that the truly happy life must be built around it (580d–583a). If you're an honor-lover, you'll balk at that conclusion, no matter how good my argument is, because it just doesn't jibe with your own experience.

AXIOTHEA: I remember Adeimantus says something like that in *Republic* 6. People dismiss Socrates' arguments, even though they can't refute them, because the conclusions don't suit them (487a–d).

LASTHENIA: Right. That's why experience matters in ethics much more than in mathematics or music.

AXIOTHEA: Fair enough. But what has all that to do with Plato's dialogues?

LASTHENIA: I'm getting to that. The thought I had was that the dialogues that deal with the virtues and how to live have more dramatic coloring not just because they're easier than the others (if indeed they are), but also because they have to deal with desires and emotions in a way that the others don't.

PLATO: Is your idea that a work on ethics must somehow or other appeal to our own feelings and emotions if it's to be successful, whereas a work on metaphysics or epistemology, like a work on mathematics, doesn't have to do that?

LASTHENIA: Sort of. . . . Again, I can't seem to get my thought into clear focus. It's something like this. I was assuming, as I think most people do, that we're meant to admire your Socrates uncritically; that he's the hero of your dialogues, the one with whom, so to speak, you identify completely. But now I'm seeing it a little differently. Maybe we're supposed to look at Socrates the way he wants us to look at other things. We're supposed to examine him and see that, though there's a lot that's admirable about him, he has faults, too. And maybe one of those faults, as I said earlier, is that he's cruel and enjoys refuting people too much.

AXIOTHEA: Oh, I get it now! By seeing the effect Socrates has on people—for example, that he doesn't, as Adeimantus points out, often succeed in convincing them of his views—we're supposed to diagnose what's wrong with his way of philosophizing. And you're claiming that that's what Plato had in mind? Well, is it, Plato? Is that how you mean us to read the dialogues?

PLATO: I'm not sure how to answer that. A book's like a child. When it's done, it has to make its own way in the world. If my dialogues are any good, they'll work the way I hoped they would. If they don't work that way, no further words of mine are likely to succeed where they failed. But although I believe that, I also believe that an author doesn't always know what his works mean, or what they're trying to do. They're inspired by the gods, and they always have more in them than their author himself can see. So you shouldn't think that *I* can answer your question, Axiothea, in some final and authoritative way. Like you, I must discover what my works mean by examining what they say.

AXIOTHEA: You're beginning to sound like a poet, Plato, not like a philosopher!

PLATO: You're more confident than I, apparently, about just how a philosopher should sound.

LASTHENIA: Well *I* think we should read the dialogues in the way I propose, not as simply idealizing Socrates, but as presenting a problematic portrait of him that's as critical as it is laudatory. I mean, just look at the *Republic* itself. It shows there's something missing in Socrates as a philosopher. Why? Because the Socrates we know and love (or hate) from dialogues like *Euthyphro* and *Crito*—the Socrates who, as Thrasymachus charges (337a), asks questions but never answers them—is found *unsatisfactory* by Glaucon and Adeimantus (358b–d, 367b–e). They want something more. And, in response to their demand, Socrates suddenly changes his spots. Instead of just asking questions and refuting the answers, he starts providing complex theories of his own—page after page of them. Could there be a more dramatic proof that you're urging us to see faults in Socrates and showing us how to correct them?

Then there's the fact—I don't know why I didn't think of it before—that while the old, familiar Socrates will examine anyone, no matter how poorly he's been educated, or how little mathematics he knows, the new Socrates restricts such examination to mature people who've had ten whole years of science. "Isn't it one lasting precaution," he says, "not to let them taste arguments while they're young?" (539a).

AXIOTHEA: You're right. Examination *has* somehow become something a lot more specialized, something for professional philosophers only. But where does all that stuff about honor-lovers and emotions and experience come in?

LASTHENIA: It's our emotional reactions to Socrates—in my case, a mixture of love and hatred—that make Plato's portrait of him problematic. It's by working through those feelings, and bringing our experiences to bear on them, that we come to love and hate the right things in him. And by doing *that*, we become philosophers ourselves. Philosophy is a matter of *loving* something, after all, and not just, as in mathematics, of being clever at proving things.

AXIOTHEA: People who aren't all that good at science and mathematics are always trying to claim some higher wisdom for themselves! But I'll let that go. Because even though I haven't lived as long as either of you and don't have your emotional maturity, I think I do see a problem both of you have missed.

PLATO: After what I've heard from Eudoxus, I wouldn't be surprised!

AXIOTHEA: Yes, well, arguments are arguments, no matter what they deal with! Anyway, here's my problem. You said earlier, Plato, that the appetitive and emotional parts of us seldom grow up completely, seldom become fully mature, and so continue to seek the satisfactions that the theater offers them. You contrasted them with the rational part of us, which you said can learn to leave such satisfactions far behind, or something like that. Later, however, in your discussion with Lasthenia, you agreed that philosophy—especially ethics and, I imagine, politics as well—required not just intelligence, or reasoning power, but emotional maturity, too. Well, you see my problem. How can reason leave the theater far behind when—according to you and Lasthenia, at any rate—

reason needs mature emotions in order to be truly philosophical and love wisdom?

PLATO: Whew, Axiothea, I don't think I know yet what to say! What about you, Lasthenia?

LASTHENIA: I'm not sure. What's coming to mind is something I dimly remember from *Republic* 10, something about the difference between the embodied soul and the disembodied one. I wonder if that might help.

PLATO: Is this what you're thinking of? When our soul is disembodied, it's simple and has only rational desires for the truth. But when it's put into our bodies, it becomes complex and acquires appetites for food, drink, and sex as well as emotional or spirited desires for honor and approval (611b–612a).

LASTHENIA: Yes, that's the passage. I was thinking that maybe reason needs mature emotions—emotions that are in harmony with reason—only when it's embodied. Odysseus is a good example (390d, 441b). His spirit urges him to kill the serving maids on the spot. But his reason tells him to delay gratification, so that he can kill the suitors as well. So his soul is in conflict. Reason wins out, in his case, because spirit listens to reason. But in other cases, where so-called weak will is involved, spirit might not listen. That's why it needs physical and musical training if it's to become reason's ally (441e–442b).

PLATO: Would that argument satisfy you, Axiothea?

AXIOTHEA: Well, I'd hardly call it an argument! I mean disembodied souls sound more like mystery religion than sober philosophy to me!

PLATO: You're still confident, I see, that you can tell what real philosophy sounds like.

AXIOTHEA: It isn't just me this time, it's you—sorry, the new Socrates—as well. Again, I'm quoting from memory, and leaving out some bits: "What we've said about the soul is true of it as it appears at present. But . . . we have to look somewhere else in order to discover its true nature . . . namely, to its love of wisdom. We must realize what it grasps and longs to have intercourse with, because it's akin to the divine and immortal and what always is, and we must realize what it would become if it followed this longing with its whole being, and if the resulting effort lifted it out of the sea in which it now dwells, and if the many stones and shells (those that have grown all over it in a wild, earthy, and stony profusion because it feasts at those so-called happy dinner parties on earth) were hammered off it. For then we'd see what its true nature is and be able to determine whether it has many parts or just one and whether, or in what manner, it is put together" (611c–612a). I mean, this makes it sound as if philosophy—the love of wisdom—hates the body, with its attendant appetites and emotions, and would pull free of it if it could and go and dwell among the forms. But if that's right, I don't see how philosophy—pure, true philosophy—can have anything to do with ethics and politics even here on Earth. Frankly, philosophy sounds more like mathematics to me: a matter for pure reason, and not for some sort of amalgam of reason and mature emotion.

LASTHENIA: You're going too fast for me!

PLATO: Is this what you have in mind? Ethics and politics deal with such virtues as justice, moderation, and courage. But these belong only to complex souls. Justice, for example, is a harmonious relationship between appetite, emotion, and reason in which all three do their own job and don't meddle with one another (441d–e). In other words, it seems that a simple soul cannot be just.

AXIOTHEA: Right. So philosophy couldn't be the love of justice or of any of the other virtues that require a complex soul.

PLATO: Because if it were, it couldn't pull the soul free of the body and make it simple rather than complex?

AXIOTHEA: Exactly. If it loved justice, and so wanted to be just, it would have to want to be complex, too. It would have to want to stay embodied and have sex with people, not rise up and have sex with the forms!

LASTHENIA: Axiothea, really! You're shameless!

AXIOTHEA: I'm just repeating what's in the *Republic*. "Longs to have intercourse with" sounds pretty sexual to me!

PLATO: Well, there is something erotic about getting hold of the truth. I'm sure you've felt it yourself when you made a discovery in geometry. What you find can be so utterly beautiful that its effect is like seeing a beautiful boy exercising naked in the gymnasium.

AXIOTHEA: A beautiful *girl*, you mean! Now, there's something the *Republic* gets right: women exercising naked in the gym!

LASTHENIA: Ugh . . . as if life weren't hard enough! Think of the competition to have the best-looking body! But let's go back to the argument for a minute. A simple soul can't be just, you say, because justice is a sort of harmony. But isn't a single note a sort of harmony, too? I mean, if a soul has only one part, aren't all its parts necessarily in harmony?

AXIOTHEA: As one might say, in mathematics, that a circle's a sort of polygon—a one-sided one!

LASTHENIA: Yes, something like that.

AXIOTHEA: But that's just not convincing. Why say that a simple soul is just, rather than neither just nor unjust, or somehow the wrong sort of thing to be either just or unjust?

LASTHENIA: Because it won't commit any unjust acts?

AXIOTHEA: Then geometrical objects will be just, too, since they don't commit any unjust acts, either! No, there's a real problem here, and you aren't facing up to it! If the soul isn't really complex, it can't really be just. And if a soul that truly loves philosophy would disembody itself if it could, and make itself simple, then true philosophy simply doesn't have any interest in justice. And . . .

LASTHENIA: I think I know what's coming next: "And if true philosophy has no interest in justice and the like, you don't really need harmonious emotions and life experience to do it; you just need the sort of intelligence that a good mathematician, like me, has."

AXIOTHEA: Exactly! True philosophers are like mathematicians. They study eternal forms. But what they study doesn't include justice, since justice is of interest only to embodied reason, not to reason pure and simple. Indeed, I suspect that you were right earlier, when you said that Sophocles and the other tragedians—and I'd include the comic writers as well—know more about us and how we should live than Socrates does. I suspect, indeed, that the question of how to live really is the sort of question that only emotionally mature people who've experienced life's vicissitudes can answer. It's a question for the theater, not the Academy!

LASTHENIA: But if that's right, then philosophers aren't the right sorts of people to be censoring the poets.

AXIOTHEA: Exactly! Socrates is always going on in the *Republic* about how people should stick to the one job for which they're naturally suited. But that doesn't stop him from sticking his nose into Homer, Hesiod, and the other poets and playwrights.[18] He should recognize that he's a philosopher, a dweller among the forms, and leave the theater to other, more earthbound spirits!

LASTHENIA: But who'll censor the poets, then, and make sure they don't corrupt people with their false views?

PLATO: Good question! Those who know the good, no doubt. But we must discuss that another day. I have to be off to see to the sacrifice in honor of Socrates. Tomorrow's the anniversary of his death, as you know, and so we must celebrate his soul's escape, just as he asked us to.

AXIOTHEA: Well, I told you we'd have fun with Plato. But look, he left his book behind. Now I can see what he was reading so secretly! My goodness, it's the *plays* of someone called Sophron![19] That old devil—I knew he liked the theater just as much as I do!

LASTHENIA: Well, maybe I *should* try to go with you next time!

AXIOTHEA: That's the spirit. I have some men's clothes I could lend you.

---

18. Hesiod (c.500 B.C.), a poet, was the author of *Theogony* and *Works and Days*.

19. Sophron of Syracuse (c.470–400 B.C.) was an author of mimes or imitative dramas, thought by some to have been precursors to Plato's dialogues. He may be alluded to at *Republic* 451c.

JUSTICE

LASTHENIA: You've only yourself to blame, Axiothea. No one forced you to drink so much wine.

AXIOTHEA: Be sweet to me! I need comforting, not scolding. I've got a terrible headache. I think I'm going to throw up at any moment.

LASTHENIA: Here, let me hold your head. My hands are nice and cool.

AXIOTHEA: Ah! That's lovely. Could you rub my neck while you're at it? My muscles are all tense. And it's partly your fault! I spent the whole night arguing with you in a dream.

LASTHENIA: What about?

AXIOTHEA: You'll laugh when I tell you.

LASTHENIA: A bit of a laugh wouldn't do either of us any harm!

AXIOTHEA: I suppose not. Before I went to the party, I said to myself, "Axiothea, you know with all that wine around, you'll be tempted to drink too much. Remember what happened to you last time. . . . This time, be moderate. Pace yourself. Drink just enough to get in the mood." Well, you know the rest. I was tired after working on some problems Eudoxus gave me. I had trouble unwinding. The first drink didn't seem to have any effect at all. So I had another right away. I still felt as sober as a judge. So I had a third. Before I knew it, I'd had six or seven. And the party hadn't even gotten into full swing! Then all six or seven hit me with a bang. I'm so weak-willed, you should call me Akrasia instead of Axiothea!

LASTHENIA: Akrasia: weakness of will. Socrates claims there's no such thing. You can't know what the best thing to do is and then not do it. That's what he says. Knowledge isn't a slave that's dragged around by desire.

29

AXIOTHEA: That's part of the argument I was having with you in my dream! There I was, suffering from weak will and its consequences and arguing at the same time about whether what I was suffering from even existed! That's what I thought would make you laugh.

LASTHENIA: You probably had to be there to appreciate the joke! What was the other part of your argument?

AXIOTHEA: Strangely enough, it was about justice, the central topic of the *Republic*. You were arguing that justice and weakness of will were somehow connected. I was resisting, but you were slowly seducing me.

LASTHENIA: You must really have been dreaming at that stage! Tell me, though, how did the first part of the argument go?

AXIOTHEA: I haven't the energy to repeat the whole thing. I'm not even sure I can remember it all. I was pretty drunk. So why don't we argue it out again together?

LASTHENIA: All right, if you really feel up to it.

AXIOTHEA: A good argument might help distract me from my misery.

LASTHENIA: Great!

AXIOTHEA: Well, we all think weak will exists. We think we've experienced it ourselves. But we also believe that "no one freely goes for bad things," that "it's not in human nature to be prepared to go for what you think to be bad in preference to what's good" or to choose the greater of two evils when you can choose the lesser.

LASTHENIA: You sound just like Plato's *Protagoras*!

AXIOTHEA: No wonder! I was probably quoting it! I read it just yesterday. Anyway, I think we all do accept that principle of rational choice. But *it*—that very principle—entails that weakness of will is impossible! I think *that's* really Socrates' point. He isn't giving us a contentious argument of his own against weakness of will. He's showing us, in characteristic Socratic fashion, that we're committed to its impossibility ourselves. That's what got me. *I* was committed to the impossibility of the very thing I was suffering from!

LASTHENIA: I see. But your impression of Socrates and mine aren't quite the same. I thought he did have a contentious argument against weakness of will and that there was something wrong with it. Let's see if I can reconstruct it for you. It's something like this. (1): The good is pleasure, and evil is pain (*Protagoras* 353c–355a). (2): Sometimes A knows that X is worse than Y but chooses X because she's overcome by desire for the pleasures of X (355a–b). In other words, A succumbs to weakness of will. Then, on the basis of (1), we substitute "less pleasant" for "worse" in (2). That gives us (3): Sometimes A knows that X is less pleasant than Y but chooses X because she's overcome by the pleasures of X. But (3) is absurd, because (4): "One must choose the more pleasant over the less, the less painful over the more" (356b).

AXIOTHEA: You sound just like my mathematician friends! They're always going on about X's and Y's and A's and B's, too! But to the extent that I follow you, I agree that that's how Socrates argues.

LASTHENIA: Well, then, he *does* have an argument against weakness of will, just as I said.

AXIOTHEA: I never claimed he didn't. I just said it wasn't contentious. I mean, your (4) is just my principle of rational choice in disguise! All you have to do is reverse the substitution you performed on (2) to get your (3)—you see, I can talk like that, too! Anyway, reverse the substitution in (4), and what do you get?

LASTHENIA: You must choose the better over the worse, the less bad over the more bad. Oh, I see, that is just your principle of rational choice!

AXIOTHEA: It isn't only mine, Lasthenia, it's yours and everyone else's, too. That's Socrates' point. Our belief in weakness of will is inconsistent with our belief in that principle.

LASTHENIA: Not so fast. Let's go back to the argument that's supposed to establish that inconsistency. I said it was contentious, and I still think that. In the first place, it isn't even valid as it stands.

AXIOTHEA: Why not?

LASTHENIA: Well, for one thing, it presupposes that the stronger desire is always for the larger pleasure, or the larger good.

AXIOTHEA: How does it do that?

LASTHENIA: Suppose A believes Y is more pleasant or better than X, but her desire for X just happens to be a lot stronger than her desire for Y.

AXIOTHEA: Oh, I see, then her desire for X would simply overpower her desire for Y, and she'd do X.

LASTHENIA: Right. And in that case she'd have succumbed to weakness of will, wouldn't she? She'd have done what she believed to be the worse of two actions.

AXIOTHEA: It certainly looks that way!

LASTHENIA: And there's an even bigger problem. You see, Socrates also presupposes that all desire is for pleasure or the good, and nothing else.

AXIOTHEA: He does?

LASTHENIA: Of course. Otherwise, A might desire X more than Y, even though she believed Y was more pleasant or better, because she might prefer X to Y for reasons having nothing to do with its pleasantness or goodness at all. Maybe X is the just thing to do, for example, and A is a just person.

AXIOTHEA: Wait a minute, this is all beginning to sound quite familiar. I think it's what I dreamed!

LASTHENIA: Then you probably know what I'm going to say next.

AXIOTHEA: I think I do. You're going to use that argument from *Republic* 4 on me—the one I could never fully understand.

LASTHENIA: I'm beginning to believe that you did dream all this! You see, you're right, that *is* what I was going to do. So why don't *you* take over and do it for me?

AXIOTHEA: I will, if you'll rub my back while I'm talking.

LASTHENIA: My own argument in exchange for a back rub? It hardly seems like a just trade. Oh, all right, roll over.

AXIOTHEA: Well, we all know that after *Republic* 1, Socrates changes his spots. He stops simply asking questions and refuting the answerer and starts putting forward arguments and theories of his own. It's such a dramatic change that some people suspect Plato's just using Socrates as a mouthpiece for his own views. Knowing Plato, it's probably not as simple as that. But there's some truth in it, I suppose. Anyway, there is, if what you said in my dream is true!

LASTHENIA: Which was?

AXIOTHEA: You said that Plato—or the Socrates who's allegedly one of his masks at that point—denies one of the presuppositions of my Socratic argument. "No one should catch us unprepared, then," he says, "or disturb us by claiming that no one has an appetite for drink but rather good drink, nor for food but for good food, since everyone's appetite is for good things" (437e–438a). His idea, apparently, is that once we allow that thirst is for drink alone, and not for good drink (by which I think he means drink that's good for you), we'll be able to see that weakness of will is possible, after all. What he does, in effect, is to show that our souls or minds are complex. We have rational desires for our overall good. They're located in what he calls the rational part of the soul, the part that calculates and weighs alternatives and wants to act for the best. But we also have desires—like thirst or hunger or sexual desire—that are blind to calculations about what's good. They just want drink or food or a nice, sexy back rub!

LASTHENIA: No flirting. This is therapy, not foreplay!

AXIOTHEA: Spoilsport! Rub just a bit lower, would you? Anyway, as I was saying, there are these other desires, which are blind or unresponsive to the good. Plato calls them appetites and assigns them to a different part of the soul, which he calls the appetitive part. Then the principle of noncontradiction comes in somehow. Oh, it's no good . . . I'm losing my train of thought. The pleasure you're giving me is overpowering my reason! You'll just have to take over the argument, too.

LASTHENIA: Oh, that *is* unfair! I'm giving everything and getting nothing!

AXIOTHEA: But you'll undo all the good you've done if you stop now!

LASTHENIA: You know I can't resist you when you make that disappointed face! Well, Plato's argument for the complexity of the soul or mind certainly is very complicated in places. So I'm not surprised that you've forgotten how it goes—or how I said it goes in your dream! But the gist of it—at least as far as I can see—is something like this (439a–e). (1): Thirst is a relation between two things, A, the person who feels the thirst, and drink—not good drink, just drink. So, (2): A, insofar as she's simply thirsty, just wants to drink, nothing else. (3): Sometimes, even though A is thirsty, she's unwilling to drink; she doesn't want to. Therefore, (4): Sometimes A simultaneously wants to drink and doesn't want to drink. (5): Wanting to drink and not wanting to drink are opposites. (6): No single thing can have opposite properties at the same time. The principle of noncontradiction you mentioned rules that out. So, (7): Wanting to drink and not wanting to drink must be located in different parts of A, different parts of A's soul. (8): A's not wanting to drink when she's thirsty is the result of her reasoning and calculating that it wouldn't be good for her to drink then. Maybe her doctor has forbidden her to drink while she's taking some drug. (9): A's wanting to drink, by contrast, has its source in bodily feelings, not in reason. So, (10): The part of A's soul that wants to drink in such situations is irrational appetite; the part of her that doesn't want to is her rational part.

AXIOTHEA: Yes, I remember now.

LASTHENIA: Then maybe you also remember how this argument rehabilitates weakness of will.

AXIOTHEA: I think I do. If A's thirst happens to be stronger than her rational desire, she'll act against her judgment of what's best and so succumb to weakness of will.

LASTHENIA: That's right. But notice Plato doesn't think A herself, or anything in her, aims at, or goes for, what she knows to be bad. After all, the thirst that leads her astray is for drink, not for what's bad. It's just that drinking happens to be bad for her at that moment.

AXIOTHEA: Why is that important?

LASTHENIA: Because if you want to appreciate the genius of Plato's argument, you have to see how cleverly he's preserved all our commonsense intuitions. We think weakness of will occurs. Of course it does. But we also think that no one voluntarily goes for what they know to be bad. No one's that silly. Yet, Socrates argues that these views are inconsistent. When we started talking, I think you agreed with him.

AXIOTHEA: That's right, I did. I *was* puzzled, though, about how he could be right, given what happened to me last night!

LASTHENIA: Well, Plato solves your puzzle for you.

AXIOTHEA: How?

LASTHENIA: By showing that one of the presuppositions of Socrates' argument is false.

AXIOTHEA: One you mentioned?

LASTHENIA: Yes.

AXIOTHEA: The one about all desire being for pleasure or the good?

LASTHENIA: Exactly. So you can see, I hope, how crucial it is. Hold on! I'm going to have to move. The sun just started to shine in my eyes, and it's dazzling me. Scoot up a bit, and I'll rub your legs.

AXIOTHEA: You're an angel! I'm almost my old self. So let's leave weakness of will behind. It reminds me of last night, and that's something I'd rather forget all about.

LASTHENIA: OK. Let's follow your dream and move on to justice.

AXIOTHEA: Here's what I can remember. I said justice, like all the other virtues, was a kind of skill, a type of expertise, sort of like geometry. It was knowing what the right thing to do is, and how to do it in the right way. Something like that.

LASTHENIA: You must have thought you were Socrates! He's famous for thinking that virtue is some kind of knowledge.[1]

AXIOTHEA: Well, you know what dreams are like—everyone in them is really somebody else in disguise! But, as I was saying, I was arguing that justice was a type of knowledge. At the same time, though, I was dividing a jug of wine between us. It was that Pamnian stuff I'm too fond of. Then you noticed that I'd given myself a much bigger glass. "You're being unjust," you said. "I know," I replied, "but I can't help it, I'm weak-willed." At that point, the birds started shrieking, and I woke up.

1. See *Charmides* 174b–176a, *Laches* 197e–199e, *Meno* 87d–89a.

LASTHENIA: No doubt it was those crows that live in the trees around Socrates' shrine! Socrates probably sent them to wake you up, so that you'd see how inconsistent you were being!

AXIOTHEA: Inconsistent! How?

LASTHENIA: Well, if you allow that weakness of will exists, so that you can know the best thing to do and not do it, then justice and the other virtues can't simply be kinds of knowledge. After all, you knew that it was best not to take the bigger glass of wine, but you took it anyway, because your appetite for it was stronger than your rational desire to divide the jug evenly between us. If knowing was enough to make you just, you couldn't have acted like that, no matter how strong your appetite was.

AXIOTHEA: No, I suppose not. In my drunken state, I must have forgotten that Socrates' doctrine about virtue being knowledge is so closely related to his doctrine about the nonexistence of weakness of will. Anyway, now that I'm sobering up I can see that one does pretty much seem to require the other. Wait a minute, though, if that's right, when Plato rehabilitates weakness of will, he ought to abandon the view that virtue is knowledge. Does he?

LASTHENIA: Maybe I can answer you with a story.

AXIOTHEA: Well, I suppose if I can tell you dreams, you can tell me stories!

LASTHENIA: When I first read the *Republic*, I couldn't get the hang of it. I couldn't really see what the overall argument was, or even that there was one. Then I got hooked on the part about the complexity of the soul we discussed earlier. Unlike a lot of the rest, it seemed like a nice, tight bit of reasoning.

AXIOTHEA: Like a proof in geometry, you mean?

LASTHENIA: Exactly. And once I'd figured it out and saw how it rescued weakness of will from Socrates' attack on it, I realized it offered me a sort of key to a lot of the rest of the *Republic*.

AXIOTHEA: How did it do that?

LASTHENIA: Well, look. If weakness of will is possible, then appetites and emotions can overpower rational desires for the overall good. Unless, that is, they've been somehow educated or trained to obey reason. If you want to make people virtuous, then, you can't just argue with them the way Socrates does; you have to start training them when they're still children. We all know that bad habits acquired in childhood are the hardest ones to break. But that means one has to provide those children with schools, teachers, proper courses of study, and so on. And one certainly won't be able to do that unless one has political power.

AXIOTHEA: Yes, and you also have to provide them with happy homes and good diets when they're infants.

LASTHENIA: Exactly. Because how one's treated and fed as an infant can have a huge impact on one's future life prospects. Imagine being born into the house of Atreus! Or being Oedipus' daughter, like poor Antigone![2]

AXIOTHEA: Right. But to prevent that sort of thing, to provide true equality of opportunity, you'd have to regulate family life far more closely than most cities do nowadays. Not just that, either, you'd have to regulate marriages. I mean, look how we breed really good horses. We don't allow just any stallion to mate with any mare. Far from it. We try to mate the best with the best. Now, we all agree that congenital weakness can have a big negative impact on children's life prospects. So we'd have to regulate marriages in order to minimize the chances of its occurring.

LASTHENIA: See, you're beginning to sound like parts of the *Republic* already—parts I have a hard time with!

AXIOTHEA: Maybe, but I'm also losing the thread of your story. Are we still talking about weakness of will?

LASTHENIA: In a way we are, because one could, I suppose, have a congenitally weak will, just as one could have a normal will that was weakened by bad upbringing. But back to my story. Suppose your appetites are so strong you can't bear to delay gratification. Then, you can't even be trained for a simple occupation, because you can't acquire even the minimal degree of psychological structure needed for that.

AXIOTHEA: Psychological structure?

2. Lasthenia's remarks refer to Aeschylus, *Oresteia* and Sophocles, *Antigone*.

LASTHENIA: Yes. Remember what Plato says about the appetitive part of the soul in *Republic* 9. He says it's "the money-loving part, because such appetites are most easily satisfied by means of money" (580e–581a). Well, if you want to earn money, you have to discipline your appetites, so they won't keep distracting you from your work. In other words, you have to replace the disorderly chaos of undisciplined appetites with some sort of order and structure.

AXIOTHEA: I see. It's just like toilet training. You have to learn to wait for the right moment!

LASTHENIA: Yes. Your desire to urinate, say, has to learn to obey your desire to please your mother. And when one desire becomes subordinate to another in that way, you have what I'm calling psychic structure.

AXIOTHEA: OK. I understand now.

LASTHENIA: People who can learn to postpone gratification, then, and become successful money-lovers, are producers in the kallipolis. In addition to appetites, however, we also have emotions. Plato calls them spirited desires and gives anger as an example (439e). People who are dominated by these desires, he says, are honor-lovers or victory-lovers (581a).

AXIOTHEA: Why does he say that?

LASTHENIA: Go back to your toilet-training example. You remember how pleased your mother was when you started to use the pot. She'd say, "That's a good girl! Mommy loves you." And she'd give you a little hug and kiss. But when you forgot and wet yourself, she'd get cross and tell you that you were getting too big to be having accidents like that. Then you'd find you'd get angry with yourself when you had an accident, and you'd berate yourself for not having more control.

AXIOTHEA: I do remember that. In fact, I still get angry with myself when I do something wrong. It's as if I were two people, or as if I had my mother somehow inside me, watching and criticizing me.

LASTHENIA: Yes, just as you did before you went to last night's party! Well, that's the origin of our desire for honor. After all, honor's a sort of approval that comes from others, and that's roughly how it's connected to anger, isn't it?

AXIOTHEA: I suppose so.

LASTHENIA: Good. Well, then, just think what sort of training and education you'd have to give someone to make him an honor-lover. Anyway, you know what Plato says it takes—all that musical and physical training, all those censored stories and poems!

AXIOTHEA: I know. He goes on and on about it until you almost want to scream!

LASTHENIA: I suppose he does a bit. But let's not lose sight of the forest for the trees. The honor-lovers, because they want approval more than money, will be less prone to certain sorts of weakness of will than the appetitive producers. And so, they'll be less prone to certain sorts of injustice.

AXIOTHEA: Why?

LASTHENIA: Money-lovers are appetitive people. They can control their appetites, but only when doing so leads to more appetitive satisfaction in the not-too-distant future. If their appetites are asked to wait too long, they'll rebel. And you know what happens then?

AXIOTHEA: The money-lovers succumb to weakness of will.

LASTHENIA: Exactly. But an honor-lover probably wouldn't succumb to it in similar circumstances, since he wants to be honored more than he wants food, drink, or sex. So he can compensate himself for the frustration of his appetites with thoughts of the honor and approval he'll get.

AXIOTHEA: I imagine good soldiers are like that. They fear dishonor even more than death, so they're willing to die if the prize is honor.

LASTHENIA: Yes, even though they won't be around to enjoy it!

AXIOTHEA: Whereas a money-lover would never do that, since money earned posthumously is no good to him. There are no pockets in the shroud!

LASTHENIA: That's one of the reasons the guardians in the kallipo-lis are honor-lovers, not appetitive people. You want your soldiers to be brave, not mercenaries who are in it only for the loot.

AXIOTHEA: What about the third group of people—the philoso-phers? How do they come into your story?

LASTHENIA: Remember that part of Homer's *Iliad* where Hector's debating about whether he should stay and fight Achilles or take refuge inside the walls of Troy? He says:

> *Now what? If I take cover inside,*
> *Polydamas will be the first to reproach me.*
> *He begged me to lead the Trojans back*
> *To the city on that black night when Achilles rose.*
> *But I wouldn't listen, and now I've destroyed*
> *Half the army through my recklessness.*
> *I can't face the Trojan men and women now,*
> *Can't bear to hear some lesser man say,*
> *"Hector trusted his strength and lost the army."*
> *That's what they'll say. I'll be much better off*
> *Facing Achilles, either killing him*
> *Or dying honorably before the city.*[3]

You see, here Hector makes a bad decision because of his love of honor. He knows he can't defeat Achilles, and that Troy will fall to the Greeks if he isn't around to protect it. So he knows the best thing to do is to take Polydamas' advice, even belatedly, and live to fight another day. But he can't do it, because he loves honor even more than he loves what's best.

AXIOTHEA: I see. So it's almost as if he's succumbing to a sort of weakness of will in which his love of honor overpowers his judg-ment about what's best for him and for Troy.

LASTHENIA: Right.

---

3. Homer, *Iliad* 22.114–25. Translated by Stanley Lombardo (Indianapo-lis: Hackett, 1997).

AXIOTHEA: Ah! Now I think I see how your story ends! The truth-loving philosophers, you'll say, have disciplined not just their appetites, but their love of honor, too, because they've subordinated both of them to their rational desire for the overall good.

LASTHENIA: Exactly! Their entire soul is so structured that their rational desires are never overpowered by their appetites or emotions.

AXIOTHEA: So they can't succumb to weakness of will and can't be unjust, is that what you're saying?

LASTHENIA: Yes. If, in order to know the good at all, you have to have a soul that's structured in the same way as a philosopher's, you can't know the good and not do it. In their case, then, virtue could be knowledge.

LASTHENIA: Well, that's pretty much the end of my story. Though, of course, I've had to leave out a lot of the details. The main point is that once you allow that weakness of will is possible, you need a much more complex psychology, a much more complex account of moral education, a much more complex picture of virtue—and, of course, a much more complex picture of the relationship between philosophy and politics.

AXIOTHEA: Explain that last bit again.

LASTHENIA: Well, Socrates is to a large extent apolitical. For him, philosophy's a sort of resident alien in the city. It's allowed to live there on sufferance. But when it runs afoul of political power, it gets suppressed.

AXIOTHEA: You're thinking about how the Athenians put him to death, aren't you?

LASTHENIA: Yes, but also about the relationship of philosophy to politics more generally. You see, if the philosophers alone have the degree of psychic structure necessary to be just—to know the good and be incapable of weakness of will—then cities will have no rest from evils "until philosophers rule as kings or those who are nowadays called kings and leading men become genuine and adequate philosophers, so that political power and philosophy become thoroughly blended together" (473c–d).

AXIOTHEA: It'll be a long time before we can expect to have that kind of rest, then! In the meantime, why don't we take a little snooze and finish our conversation when we wake up? Here, you can lie down next to me, and I'll stroke your hair until you fall asleep.

LASTHENIA: My older sister used to do that. I've never been able to say no to it.

AXIOTHEA: You told me.

FORMS

AXIOTHEA: My god, Aristotle, what *is* that?

ARISTOTLE: It's a copy of the *Republic*.

AXIOTHEA: Not that, idiot, the thing crawling on your arm!

ARISTOTLE: It's a beetle I'm studying. What does it look like?

AXIOTHEA: I don't know. It's too disgusting to look at, all black and shiny. It's giving me the creeps. Can't you put it somewhere else?

ARISTOTLE: You mathematicians! You think only nice, clean, abstract things are worth studying. But if you want to be a true philosopher, you have to study beetles. The gods have an enormous fondness for them, you know. There are probably more species of beetles than of anything else.

AXIOTHEA: Ugh! Don't tell me that! Give me perfection. That's what the gods really love. They're perfect themselves, and so they love perfection. They don't love bronze spheres, like this one, which change and decay and are only roughly spherical. What they love is the form of a sphere, which is perfectly spherical and never changes. Beautiful girls don't turn their heads; only beauty itself, the unchanging perfectly beautiful form of beauty, does.

ARISTOTLE: Plato says the same sort of thing in here. But those perfect things aren't alive. They're embalmed, frozen, dead.

AXIOTHEA: Oh my god! That beetle of yours is crawling on *me* now, I can feel it. I wish *it* were dead!

ARISTOTLE: It's probably just eating your dead skin. It likes that. Here, I'll take it.

AXIOTHEA: Why do you bother with such things?

ARISTOTLE: My father was a doctor, you know. When I was a boy, he used to talk to me about human bodies and how they work. Sometimes he'd even let me watch him examining patients. I've actually seen babies being born. I'll bet you haven't. It's fascinating. Babies inherit traits from both their parents. I wish I knew how it's managed! Anyway, all of that got me interested in animals. They're a lot like us. They move around, perceive their environment, reproduce. Ants and bees even live in something like cities. Some animals are incredibly ingenious, too. I once saw ants crawl up to the top of a piece of grass so as to bend it over a stream. Then the rest of the colony used it as a bridge. You won't catch your beloved forms and numbers doing anything as smart as that!

AXIOTHEA: Maybe not. But you won't find any of your ants doing geometry, either. That takes reason, and other animals just don't have it. So really, when you come down to it, we're very different from them. As for babies, I don't want anything to do with them—messy, noisy things!

ARISTOTLE: I agree: we're different from ants. But even reason is something we inherit from our parents, so it must somehow be biological; it must be some sort of life or life function. I don't have a good account of it worked out. Reason's hard.

AXIOTHEA: I don't see how our reason can come from our parents. I think it comes from the gods. It's just not like other things. It's not even human, really, but divine. It's like the things it studies best, like the perfect sphere, perfect beauty, or perfect justice.

ARISTOTLE: Maybe so. But beetles are pretty amazing, too. This one has a far keener sense of smell than any human. It can smell rotting flesh from an enormous distance.

AXIOTHEA: Oh, for goodness sake! Stop talking about dead things! I want to talk to you about the forms.

ARISTOTLE: Those paradigms of life! What do you want to say about them?

AXIOTHEA: *I* don't want to say anything, I want to hear *your* views. Lasthenia told me you don't believe in them. If that's true, you won't last long here!

ARISTOTLE: Nonsense. Plato likes criticism. He doesn't want to be surrounded by a lot of little Platonists! Dialectic can't flourish if everyone's saying the same thing.

AXIOTHEA: That's not the impression I get from that book you're carrying. In the ideal city described there, everyone sings the same song. But have it your own way! Just remember, Plato's getting old, and not everyone's as tolerant as he is. We'd better watch out, though, or we'll be discussing Academic politics, instead of metaphysics, and I avoid that like the plague! So . . . what's wrong with forms?

ARISTOTLE: Maybe you ought to tell me first just what you mean by forms.

AXIOTHEA: Should I stick to the *Republic* and what I think Plato means by them there?

ARISTOTLE: If you want to.

AXIOTHEA: Well, he first mentions forms in *Republic* 3. He says we won't be educated "until we know the different forms of moderation, courage, generosity, high-mindedness, and all their kindred, and their opposites too, which are scattered around everywhere, and see them in the things in which they are" (402c). But those forms—kinds might be better—aren't the ones I'm talking about. I'm talking about Forms, with a capital 'F', so to speak. The forms or kinds of moderation are *many*, and are *visible* in the various things we see around us. But the Form of moderation, for example, or of justice or anything else, is a single, unique, intelligible thing, not a visible one. It's something we see with the intellect, not with the physical eye: "The many beauties and the rest are visible but not intelligible, while the Forms are intelligible but not visible" (507b). Forms of the sort I'm talking about don't really appear until *Republic* 5. There Plato (or Socrates; I won't bother to distinguish them) introduces his philosophers for the first time. He says, "Since beautiful is the opposite of ugly, they are two things," and "since they are two things, each of them is also *one*." Then he goes on to claim, "The same argument applies to just and unjust, good and bad, and *all the Forms*: each of them is itself one thing, but because they associate all over the place with actions and bodies, and with one another, each of them *appears to be many*" (475e–476a).

ARISTOTLE: I have the passage in front of me.

AXIOTHEA: Right. Well, the philosophers, he says, are the ones who "in each case study the things themselves that are always the same in every respect"—in other words, the Forms. As a result, "they have knowledge," he claims, "not mere belief" (479e).

ARISTOTLE: Exactly.

AXIOTHEA: He contrasts the philosophers with people he calls "sight-lovers" and "craft-lovers," who acknowledge the existence of what he calls "the many beauties" (478e–479b)—by which, I think, he means the many (small 'f') forms or kinds of beauty visible with the physical eye in the things scattered around us (476a)—but whose "thought is unable to see the nature of the beautiful itself or be passionately devoted to it" (476b). As a result, he says, they "have beliefs about all these things but have no knowledge of what their beliefs are about" (479e).

ARISTOTLE: I agree. That's what he does, all right. So far, though, you've mentioned only Forms of beauty, moderation, justice, and the like. Are those the only sorts of Forms you think there are—Forms of virtue and other such valuable things?

AXIOTHEA: No, not at all. There are Forms of big and small, light and heavy, double and half (479a–b).

ARISTOTLE: Yes, but those are a bit out of the ordinary as well. They aren't plain old material objects like chairs and tables. What I want to know is whether you think there are Forms of them.

AXIOTHEA: I do. There's something about that at the beginning of *Republic* 10. Give me the book for a second, and I'll look it up.

ARISTOTLE: Here you are. I've marked the passage!

AXIOTHEA: I'm not surprised. We all know our *Republic* here! Anyway, let me read it: "We customarily hypothesize a single Form in connection with each of the many things to which we apply the same term." Apparently, then, there's a Form corresponding to every term.

ARISTOTLE: To every *general* term, you mean? Or do you think there's a Form corresponding to the name 'Aristotle' or 'Axiothea'?

AXIOTHEA: No, of course there isn't. I meant, as I think Plato did, that there's a Form corresponding to every general term. The examples he goes on to give are 'couch' and 'table' (596b).

ARISTOTLE: Let's assume that's right, then. Though it worries me that Plato says only that we "*hypothesize* a single Form" for each general term.

AXIOTHEA: Why does that worry you?

ARISTOTLE: Because he says that to turn a hypothesis into something unhypothetical, you have to refute all the objections that can be brought against it (437a, 538b–c).

AXIOTHEA: You mean we start by assuming that there's a Form corresponding to every general term, but we'd give up that assumption if we ran into objections we couldn't answer?

ARISTOTLE: Well, I'm really just voicing a worry and being cautious. So why don't we, too, just hypothesize that there's a Form corresponding to every general term? That way, we won't beg any questions.

AXIOTHEA: OK.

ARISTOTLE: Well, we know a bit about what Forms are now: they're unique, unchanging, intelligible objects that correspond to general terms and that philosophers alone can countenance. But you haven't said yet why we should suppose there are such things, though you've implied that it has something to do with knowledge.

AXIOTHEA: That's right. Plato thinks that if you don't countenance Forms, you can have belief but you can't have knowledge.

ARISTOTLE: Why does he do that?

AXIOTHEA: He's not very clear about it, in my view. But this passage seems to contain the nub of his argument: "Now that all that has been established, I want him to tell me this—the excellent fellow who believes that there's no beautiful itself, no form of beauty itself that remains always the same in all respects, but who does believe that there are many beautiful things. I mean—that lover of sights who cannot bear to hear anyone say that the beautiful is one thing, or the just, or any of the rest—I want him to answer this question. 'My good fellow,' we'll say, 'of all the many beautiful things, is there one that won't also seem ugly? Or any just one that won't seem unjust? Or any pious one that won't seem impious?'" (478e–479a)

ARISTOTLE: I agree, that does seem to be the crucial part. I take it you'd spell it out something like this. Suppose Socrates asks you what justice is. And what he wants is a standard or paradigm that will enable him to tell in a wholly correct and reliable way which things are just and which aren't. And suppose you answer that justice is paying back what one owes. Then he'll object that while it's sometimes just to pay back what one owes, it's also sometimes unjust to do so. For example, it's unjust to return a sword you've borrowed to someone who's now out of his mind (331b–c). Hence, if Socrates were to use *your* account of justice as a standard or paradigm, then his judgment about what particular acts were just wouldn't be reliable. It would be sometimes right and sometimes wrong. Hence, he wouldn't have knowledge about justice or what things are just, since knowledge must always be right, and so must involve reliable standards of judgment.

AXIOTHEA: Right. What he'd have would just be belief, since belief, unlike knowledge, is sometimes true and sometimes false.

ARISTOTLE: Forms, then, are introduced to avoid that problem.

AXIOTHEA: Right, again. Unlike giving back what one owes, which is no more just than unjust, the Form of justice is perfectly just and in no way unjust. If you use it as your standard, therefore, you'll never call something just that's unjust, or vice versa.

ARISTOTLE: And the Forms are the stock-in-trade of the philosophers, because philosophy is the love of wisdom, wisdom is a type of knowledge, and knowledge requires Forms?

AXIOTHEA: Exactly! So now are you ready to tell me what's wrong with Forms?

ARISTOTLE: It's not as easy as that. I haven't got everything worked out yet. I haven't a book about the Forms ready for you to read. All I have are a few thoughts and bits of argument I'm still mulling over.

AXIOTHEA: Like what?

ARISTOTLE: Well, here's one I've actually tried out on Plato. He was pretty impressed with it, but it didn't knock him dead in the way I hoped it would. He just said it was very interesting and that he'd think about it!

AXIOTHEA: Great! Start with that one, then.

ARISTOTLE: You, Plato, and Speusippus are all men.[1] But you're all moving and changing. You all came into being at birth and will cease to be at death. So none of you is the eternal, immutable Form of a man. I'm assuming there is one, since 'man' is clearly a general term.

AXIOTHEA: Right so far.

ARISTOTLE: Now, why are you all men? What makes you men?

AXIOTHEA: We all resemble—or participate in—the Form of a man (476c–d).

ARISTOTLE: Right. But in what respect? I mean everything resembles everything else in some way. You resemble this beetle, for example. You're both alive, you both move by yourselves, you both perceive your environment, and so on. But you're not both beetles, or both men.

AXIOTHEA: That's the first time anyone's ever said that I resemble a beetle! But you're right, of course. What makes me a man is that I resemble the Form of a man in having the qualities definitive of men, the ones that determine what it is to be a man in the first place.

ARISTOTLE: Exactly. So, then, the Form of a man must have those qualities, too, mustn't it?

AXIOTHEA: Of course it must, since it resembles me in having them.

ARISTOTLE: And anything that has those qualities is a man, isn't it?

AXIOTHEA: Yes, since they're the very ones that determine what it is to be a man.

ARISTOTLE: So the Form of a man is a man?

---

1. Speusippus (c.407–339 B.C.), Athenian philosopher, was the son of Plato's sister Potone. He took over the headship of the Academy on Plato's death.

AXIOTHEA: Yes, it is. I could have told you that at the beginning. The Form of a sphere, which is perfectly spherical, is a sphere, too, and the Form of justice is perfectly just. There's nothing strange about that.

ARISTOTLE: Fair enough! But when I asked why you and Plato and Speusippus were men, you said it was because you resembled the Form of a man.

AXIOTHEA: I did.

ARISTOTLE: And you were making a general point, weren't you? You were saying or implying that *anything* that's a man is a man because it resembles that Form?

AXIOTHEA: Yes, that's right.

ARISTOTLE: Now, if I told you that A, B, and C were men because each of them resembled A in being a man, you'd rightly accuse me of giving a circular explanation, wouldn't you?

AXIOTHEA: I certainly would.

ARISTOTLE: So if I told you that you, Plato, Speusippus, and X were all men because each of you resembled X in being a man, you'd say the very same thing.

AXIOTHEA: Absolutely.

ARISTOTLE: Well, then, put in the Form of a man for X, just as you would in a mathematical equation, and see what happens.

AXIOTHEA: Then I wouldn't be able to explain why Plato, Speusippus, X, and myself were all men by appealing to their resemblance to the Form of a man, since it is just X.

ARISTOTLE: Right.

AXIOTHEA: But that's not what I did. I didn't include the Form of a man in with Plato, Speusippus, and myself. So I wasn't covertly explaining why it was a man by appeal to that very fact.

ARISTOTLE: I think you were. Since you agreed that the Form of a man was itself a man, and that your explanation of why you and Plato and Speusippus were men was a *general* one, that's precisely what you were doing.

AXIOTHEA: That's clever! And you're right, of course. But that's only because I wasn't sufficiently explicit. You see, I should have made it even clearer that the Form that explains why a group of men are men can't itself be a member of the group. Otherwise, you're right—I'd be going around in circles.

ARISTOTLE: Well, there are worse fates than that. Consider Plato, Speusippus, and yourself. Suppose that you're all men because you resemble X.

AXIOTHEA: So X is the Form of a man, then?

ARISTOTLE: Call it the *first* Form of a man, if that's all right.

AXIOTHEA: OK.

ARISTOTLE: Now, X is a man, too, isn't it?

AXIOTHEA: Yes, it has to be; otherwise, we three wouldn't resemble it in the requisite way.

ARISTOTLE: Well, then, why are you, Plato, Speusippus, and X all men? Mustn't it be by resembling some *second* Form of a man, Y, to which none of you is identical? Didn't you say that what explained why the members of a group were all men couldn't itself be a member of that group or your explanation would be circular?

AXIOTHEA: I did, yes.

ARISTOTLE: Good. Now, consider you, Plato, Speusippus, X, *and* Y. You're all men. But why? Mustn't it be by resembling some *third* Form of a man—some *third man*? Well, you can probably see how the argument goes from there. You used to have a circular explanation; now you have an infinite, vicious regress, and no explanation at all!

AXIOTHEA: That's brilliant, Aristotle! You should call it the Third Man Argument! It's made me feel dizzy, in any case, the way mathematical proofs do when they seem to establish something contrary to what you've always believed. There's just one thing, though. Consider the case of spheres for a minute. There are no perfect spheres here on earth. You can't draw one, and you can't make one, not even out of the smoothest bronze. Yet, we call some earthly things spheres. For example, we call this a sphere. And we do so, it seems, because it resembles something that really is perfectly spherical, namely, the Form of a sphere. Here, there surely is a genuine explanation of some sort, though I don't quite know how to make that clear. Maybe this comes close: the shape an earthly object has is sphericality, because it (imperfectly) resembles the shape of the perfect sphere. But the latter shape is sphericality not because it (imperfectly) resembles the shape of some second Form of a sphere, but because it perfectly resembles—is identical to—sphericality itself. This account isn't circular, because I'm explaining why *imperfect* spheres are spheres by appeal to why *perfect* spheres are, and I'm giving a different explanation of the latter. There!

ARISTOTLE: Hmm! You should ask Plato what he thinks of that. My own views are complicated. I don't think I should attempt a complete diagnosis of where the problem lies. Instead, I'll try something quicker. Go back to the case of a man. If your response is to work for it, the Form of a man (the very first one) must be a perfect man. Right?

AXIOTHEA: Yes.

ARISTOTLE: But the Form of a man must be unmoving.

AXIOTHEA: Yes.

ARISTOTLE: Then we have the beetle problem! Like beetles, men are essentially alive, essentially moving and changing. They're born and they die. They reproduce. The Form of a man can't do any of those things, so it can't possibly be the perfect man.

AXIOTHEA: Somehow that seems like a cheap shot. All the same, I'm not sure how to deflect it.

ARISTOTLE: You see, there is a problem about excluding beetles— or, anyway, perfect beetles—from philosophical consideration!

AXIOTHEA: Maybe so. Like Plato, I'll have to think about it. But tell me, are those the only difficulties you have with Forms?

ARISTOTLE: No, no, I have lots more.

AXIOTHEA: Like what?

ARISTOTLE: Consider resemblance. You resemble the Form of a man. This beetle resembles the Form of a beetle. That bronze sphere you're carrying resembles the Form of a sphere. Right?

AXIOTHEA: Yes.

ARISTOTLE: So we have three different examples of one thing—resemblance—and one general term—'resemblance'—that applies to all three?

AXIOTHEA: Again, yes.

ARISTOTLE: As in the case of the group of men, therefore, can't we ask why all three are instances of that one thing?

AXIOTHEA: We can. And the reason is the same: they're all examples of resemblance, because they all resemble the Form of resemblance!

ARISTOTLE: Good!

AXIOTHEA: I don't like the satisfied way you said that. I feel I've just fallen into one of Socrates' dialectical traps.

ARISTOTLE: You have! Because I don't see now that you've gotten to the heart of resemblance. One sign of this is that the notion of resemblance has reappeared in your explanation: these three are examples of resemblance, because they all *resemble* the Form of resemblance.

AXIOTHEA: But isn't that just the charge of circularity you brought against me earlier in the case of men? And I suppose if I try to escape it in the same way, you'll trot out the Third Man again!

ARISTOTLE: Well, I could do that, of course. However, I'm actually trying to get at something a bit different, something that hinges on the fact that resemblance—unlike man or sphere—is a *relation*. But I see I'm not doing a great job of it. Let me try again. First, though, I want you to notice that relations do seem quite different from the things that stand in them, the so-called relata, and that Plato's theory of Forms doesn't seem to be able to capture that difference, since it, as we've seen, treats man, sphere, and resemblance in essentially the same way.

AXIOTHEA: I agree. But I don't see quite where you're going with it.

ARISTOTLE: Well, suppose I tell you that the handle is attached to the cup with glue. If glue were just the same sort of thing as a handle or a cup, you could then ask me how the handle is connected to the glue, the glue to the cup, and so on.

AXIOTHEA: I see. You're saying that just as glue has to be somehow different from a handle or a cup if it's to connect one to the other, so a relation like resemblance has to be different from a man or the Form of a man if it's to connect one to the other?

ARISTOTLE: Exactly. The picture I'm working with—though it's still very crude and undeveloped—is something like this. A particular object, like a man or a Form, is like that bronze sphere of yours. It can't glue things to one another. But a relation is somehow sticky. It can glue things together. It isn't an object, in other words, but something quite different.

AXIOTHEA: I'm still not sure I understand.

ARISTOTLE: Well, I said it was crude. But let me go on a bit further. If you agree with me about relations, you should also agree that there's an important way in which man and sphere are just like them. I mean, consider the analogy again. Suppose the glue had only one sticky side. It could stick itself to the handle or to the cup! So it still isn't like them, is it?

AXIOTHEA: No, it isn't.

ARISTOTLE: Well, man and sphere are sort of like that, too. Why? Because man can stick itself to particular men, like you or me, and sphere can stick itself to particular spheres, like that one? If it were otherwise, then you and I couldn't be men, and that sphere couldn't be a sphere.

AXIOTHEA: Is this your idea: we shouldn't think we need glue with two sticky sides to start the process of joining things together, since we can in fact start by, as it were, joining one thing to glue with one sticky side?

ARISTOTLE: Yes, that's sort of it. Resemblance comes in one step too late and then doesn't solve the problem. For once you have to admit glue of any sort, you might as well start with the simplest sort of glue!

AXIOTHEA: I think we're in danger of getting stuck ourselves!

ARISTOTLE: Yes, philosophical problems often seem just like sticking points in our understanding that prevent our thought from moving forward.

AXIOTHEA: Right! And dialectic is what helps us get unstuck! But if man and sphere aren't objects, what are?

ARISTOTLE: You and I are, of course, and that sphere is. We're nonsticky, we can't stick to other objects. But man, sphere, resemblance, and so on are different in that they can. Plato's problem, I think, is that he's blind to that difference. He doesn't know how to deal with the sticky things, so he treats them as if they're just like the familiar nonsticky ones—only perfect, eternal, unchanging. He's like those people who think that gods are just like humans, only eternal!

AXIOTHEA: Don't tell me you're condescending to *Plato*, of all people!

ARISTOTLE: God forbid! Plato's such a great thinker that base men shouldn't even be allowed to praise him! No, no . . . the problem posed by these sticky things is really hard. No one should be mocked for not having solved it. But let me take one more step, just so you'll see where my thoughts have been leading me.

AXIOTHEA: Go right ahead. But before you do, I think I should tell you that I already see a problem with your view. I mean, why shouldn't I think that you and that sphere are the sticky things, that the Forms are the nonsticky ones, and that it's you that needs to be stuck to them in order to exist, not them to you. I mean, what would you be if you weren't stuck to the Form of a man? Why, you wouldn't be anything at all!

ARISTOTLE: Actually, what I was going to say is sort of related to that. Plato makes objects—things, like you, me, and that sphere (I don't know where the beetle's gone!)—depend for their existence on the Forms. If the Form of a man didn't exist, particular men couldn't. But even if there were no particular men around, the Form of a man would still exist.

AXIOTHEA: That's my view, too.

ARISTOTLE: It is? But doesn't it get things the wrong way around? Surely, the sticky things should depend on the nonsticky ones, not vice versa? If there were no red things, redness wouldn't exist. It depends on them; they don't depend on it.

AXIOTHEA: When you put it that way, it sounds right. But I think the analogy may be misleading you. After all, the nonsticky things also depend on the sticky ones. Things have to have some qualities and stand in some relations. They can't just exist devoid of all properties. Maybe things don't have to be red, but they do have to have some color, shape, or texture, or what have you.

ARISTOTLE: Fair enough. But if the dependence between nonsticky things and sticky ones, between particulars and Forms, is symmetrical, if one depends on the other, then Plato's still wrong, since he thinks the dependence is asymmetrical, that particulars depend on Forms, but not vice versa. I must say, though, I still feel that the very idea of sphericality existing, but not in anything, or of resemblance existing, but not between any particular things . . . well, it just seems somehow crazy to me. Things just can't be that way. If there were no particular things, no nonsticky things, there just couldn't be any Forms!

AXIOTHEA: It must be the influence of those beetles! For even I'm inclined to think that if there were no beetles, there'd be no beetleness. But maybe that's because I've a hard time allowing that the Form of a beetle could exist in a perfect realm!

ARISTOTLE: Right! It might start crawling on the Form of a man; and then what would become of perfection?

AXIOTHEA: Very funny! Notice, however, that this new argument of yours still seems to rely on the idea that it's the Forms that are sticky and in need of something to stick to. But I pointed out earlier that we could just as well attribute stickiness to you and me and this sphere, and not to the Forms. I agree that if two things are to be joined, at least one of them must be sticky, but I don't see yet that you've shown why the Forms have to be the sticky ones.

ARISTOTLE: Well, if we look at things very abstractly, we do seem to have two options—two places we could put the stickiness, not just one. But when we get down to the concrete details, one of those options becomes vastly more attractive than the other. You see, if the Form of a man is a man, and the Form of a beetle is a beetle, and if Forms are nonsticky and don't need things like you and me and that beetle (wherever it is) for their existence, there could be men and beetles, even though nothing's alive. And that seems wildly counterintuitive to me.

AXIOTHEA: That's why it's better to leave beetles—and men—out of the picture and stick to numbers and the Forms of mathematical objects, like the perfect sphere.

ARISTOTLE: I don't think philosophers are allowed to leave things out like that. Their theories are supposed to fit reality, not the other way around!

AXIOTHEA: Oh, I didn't mean leave them out in that sense. We need some account of them. I don't deny that. I meant narrow the scope of the theory of Forms to things like the perfect sphere, numbers, ideal beauty, and other such eternal and immutable things.

ARISTOTLE: I wonder if you can.

AXIOTHEA: What do you mean?

ARISTOTLE: Well, whatever the perfect sphere is, it has to be the sort of thing that we can know, doesn't it? And the same goes for numbers and the rest?

AXIOTHEA: Of course.

ARISTOTLE: So the theory of Forms has to be able to account for our knowledge of such things?

AXIOTHEA: Yes.

ARISTOTLE: Suppose I'm sitting on a chair at noon and not sitting on it an hour later. Then the chair has changed, hasn't it, sometime between noon and one o'clock?

AXIOTHEA: Yes, it's changed from being sat on by you to not being sat on by you.

ARISTOTLE: Well, suppose at noon I'm contemplating the Form of a sphere, but an hour later I'm not. Then, hasn't the Form, like the chair, changed sometime between noon and one o'clock?

AXIOTHEA: Oh dear! I suppose it has changed—from being contemplated by you to not being contemplated by you.

ARISTOTLE: If Forms are knowable, then, they're not unchanging, and if they're unchanging, they're not knowable.

AXIOTHEA: You should try that argument on Plato, too. It's really clever.

ARISTOTLE: I have already. But as in the case of what you called the Third Man, he didn't just fall down and die!

AXIOTHEA: Thank goodness for that! I wonder if maybe he noticed that the sort of change Forms must undergo in order to be known seems somehow innocuous? It's like the change I undergo when I become smaller than you, not because my height has changed, but because you've grown taller. Somehow, it's not a real change at all. I must admit, though, that I don't see how to develop the point or explain just what a real change is.

ARISTOTLE: There's something in what you're saying. But let's leave its elaboration for later, since there's another point I want to make that has some bearing on it.

AXIOTHEA: Go ahead.

ARISTOTLE: If the theory of Forms has to be able to account for our knowledge of Forms—indeed, for our knowledge of the very theory of them itself—then it must acknowledge the existence of minds or souls, since it's exclusively by means of them that we know anything. But, now, minds and souls aren't Forms. They're living things that seem to undergo the apparently more robust sort of change you just called real change. Moreover, if the theory of Forms must also explain why, in addition to Forms, there are particular instances of them, like you and me and that beetle, then it also apparently needs some kind of divine being—some other living, changing non-Form—to produce them. For Forms alone can't do anything like make copies of themselves—they're unchanging, remember.

AXIOTHEA: My goodness, Aristotle, it has gotten late! Why, the sun's just about to set. There . . . it's gone completely. I feel as if I've suddenly become surrounded by the walls of a dark cave.

ARISTOTLE: I know. I'll never find that beetle now! I'll have to study something else until I can find another.

AXIOTHEA: At least mathematicians never have that problem—the things they study don't move around. Let's talk again soon, when I've had a chance to think things over.

FREEDOM

AXIOTHEA: Have you ever been to Phlius, Plato?

PLATO: No, I haven't.

AXIOTHEA: I didn't think so. It's in the Peloponnese, north of Mycenae, not far from the Gulf of Corinth. In 379, about six years after you founded the Academy, its democratic government was overthrown by Sparta and a narrow oligarchy was installed in its place. Democratic freedoms were soon a thing of the past. Most women weren't especially bothered by this, of course, since they'd never known much freedom anyway. But I found it intolerable. My mother, you see, wasn't from Phlius. Like Aspasia,[1] she was from the Milesian coast of Asia Minor and was my father's mistress, not his wife. She was well educated, as such women often are, and presided over a sort of salon for wandering intellectuals. One day, one of them brought her a copy of the *Republic*, which was then your latest work. She read it avidly, particularly admiring your views about women. She decided there and then that I should be given an education fitted to my abilities, not to my gender. I proved to be a good student, and when I reached the age of seventeen, she used her connections to persuade you to let me come and study here. My father, who never paid much attention to his illegitimate daughter, made no objection to my leaving. And off I went.

Imagine my exhilaration at leaving my backwater town for a great city, which enjoyed more freedoms than Phlius ever had, even when it was a democracy! The first thing I did—I almost blush to tell you—was to throw away my women's clothes and dress like a man. You see, I was determined to start my new life as my true self. In Phlius, that would have caused a sensation. Here, no one seemed to notice or care. With some of the money

---

1. Aspasia was the Milesian-born mistress of the Athenian democratic political leader, Pericles, from c.445 B.C.

my mother gave me, I bought myself a slave girl at a local brothel. She was divine. I'd never tasted so sweet a pleasure before. Two days later, I walked through the portal of the Academy. I took the entrance exam in geometry and was allowed to stay. The world has never looked the same to me. I read, think, listen to lectures, discuss my ideas with others. I live much as I want. I'm free, Plato, and in a way I owe it all to your *Republic*!

PLATO: What a story, Axiothea! Little did I think when I wrote the *Republic* that it would lead a young woman to dress like a man and engage in unnatural sexual practices!

AXIOTHEA: But I assumed from reading your works that you were somewhat unnaturally inclined yourself! Otherwise, I'd never have been so frank and open. I didn't expect to shock you. Surely, you don't think that some forms of sexual love are wrong? Isn't *erôs*, in all its forms, one of the greatest human goods? Didn't Socrates say that one of the best things about being human is that humans are in heat all year long?

PLATO: Shh! If anyone hears us talking about such things, I'll be prosecuted for corrupting the youth.

AXIOTHEA: I'm sorry. I really am. I thought that you, at least, were a free, sexually liberated man. You love boys. Your dialogues make that clear. I assumed you'd be quite open about it.

PLATO: Leave me out of it! My private life is precisely that—private. Let's talk about philosophy and leave sex in the darkness, where it belongs. Tell me, instead, about this freedom you value so highly. What is it? And why do you think it's so important?

AXIOTHEA: Freedom is being able to do what you want, Plato. And as to what's important about it, isn't that obvious? Just consider how bad *not* being able to do what you want is! If I hadn't been free to leave Phlius, I'd never have known real love or real sexual fulfillment. I'd never have known all I've learned here in the Academy. Outside of a free city like Athens, would you yourself have been free to spend your life studying philosophy, or to found the Academy? Yet, in the *Republic*, you restrict people's freedom intolerably. I certainly wouldn't want to live there. I'd have to have sex with men and have children by them, too. I wouldn't be able to read Homer or Sophocles or Aristophanes.

I wouldn't be able to eat Attic pastries or have Corinthian girl-friends (404d). Life would be so impoverished without these things—things I'm free to enjoy here in Athens—that it would scarcely be worth living.

PLATO: What about bad desires, Axiothea? What if someone desires to torture or rape you? Should he be free to do so?

AXIOTHEA: No, of course he shouldn't.

PLATO: What if one of your own desires limits your freedom to satisfy another one? What if your desire for Attic pastries makes you fat, so that Corinthian girls won't find you attractive? What if staying up late with such girls makes you too muzzy-headed to do geometry? Mustn't your freedom to satisfy some of your desires be restricted, so that you can satisfy others you think are more important?

AXIOTHEA: I suppose so.

PLATO: Even a freedom-lover like yourself, then, thinks *some* limits must be imposed on people's freedom.

AXIOTHEA: Yes. But *I* want to be the one to decide how my freedom's limited. I don't want *someone else* making my decisions for me. My life is *mine*. *I* want to decide how to live it. If I want to go to a brothel and buy myself a pretty Corinthian girl for an evening's pleasure, I want to be free to do it. If I want to study geometry in my room for days on end, I want to be free to do that, too. If I want to say no to Attic pastries, so that I'll be more able to study or seduce, I want to be the one to say it. I don't want someone else making up my mind for me.

PLATO: Not even if he knows better what's good for you than you do?

AXIOTHEA: No, not even then. Freedom and self-determination are too valuable to be traded for other goods.

PLATO: Do you feel the same way when you do geometry? Do you think that when you're trying to solve a problem about squares or triangles, you should be free to do whatever you want? Or do you think that—in this case, at least—freedom must bow to knowledge and truth?

AXIOTHEA: Well, I agree, of course, that in geometry I'm not free. There I'm constrained by the truth. I must perform the proof correctly, or it'll be no good. There's no room for personal freedom there. But life isn't like geometry. There's an absolute truth about how the radius of a circle is related to its circumference, or about how many right angles the three angles of a triangle equal. But there's no absolute truth about what the best life is, or about any other human values. That's why there are experts in geometry, but none in ethics or politics. In life, each must work out his destiny for himself. In life, there's no truth, just *my* truth and *your* truth.

PLATO: That's an old story, Axiothea. Protagoras was saying that sort of thing long before you were born.[2]

AXIOTHEA: Some old stories are true, Plato.

PLATO: Do you mean true for you, Axiothea, or absolutely true?

AXIOTHEA: It's true, Plato, absolutely true, that values are all relative to the individual, and none are absolute.

PLATO: But that's a claim about values. And didn't you say earlier that there were *no* absolute truths about them?

AXIOTHEA: I did. But I spoke carelessly. I should have said that it's true *for me* that all values are relative and none absolute.

PLATO: But it's not true *for me*. You see, I do think that some things are absolutely good and absolutely bad, regardless of people's opinions. Am I wrong?

AXIOTHEA: Of course you're wrong. Didn't I just claim the opposite?

PLATO: You did at first. You said that it was absolutely true that values are all relative to the individual, and none are absolute. Under questioning, however, you changed your mind. You claimed that it was true only *for you* that values were all relative to the individual. Then I claimed that it's true *for me* that they aren't relative in that way. But now you see we're not disagreeing,

2. Protagoras of Abdera (c.490–420 B.C.), a famous sophist, or intinerant professor of rhetoric and philosophy. "Man," he famously said, "is the measure of all things"—meaning that beliefs and perceptions are all true for the person who has them.

because what's not true for you may well be true for me. Isn't that the whole point of adding 'for me' and 'for you' to 'true'?

AXIOTHEA: Yes. You're right. I shouldn't have said that you're wrong about values. You have your truth about them. I have mine. That's all there is to it.

PLATO: So we shouldn't really be arguing about values, should we? Or be trying to change each other's opinions by giving reasons? For reasons are reasons to believe that something's *true*. Since all truth about values is relative, according to you, reasons relevant to values must be relative, too. My reasons won't be reasons *for you*, then, unless we happen to agree about values. So if I want to persuade you to change your views, all I can do, it seems, is bamboozle you or get you to feel differently by using rhetoric to arouse your passions, or twist your arm until you agree to value what I do. I can *force* you to change your views, in other words, but I can't rationally persuade you to do so.

AXIOTHEA: That's right. All so-called reasoning about values is just a power struggle. Victory goes to the more persuasive speaker or the more powerful side. Reason and truth don't come into it.

PLATO: But didn't you come here to discuss the *Republic* with me? Didn't you come to criticize what it says about values, to explain to me what was wrong with it, or to be given reasons to change your own mind? Now, however, it seems that you really came either to twist my arm or to use rhetoric to bend me to your will.

AXIOTHEA: Oh but, Plato, even you've got to admit that ethics is different from geometry, or astronomy, or any of the sciences! I mean, geometry's the same everywhere, and so is astronomy. A proof either works or it doesn't. But justice and other values differ from place to place. Herodotus shows that in his *Histories*.[3] He agrees with Pindar that convention is king of all.[4]

---

3. Herodotus of Halicarnassus (c.480/490–425 B.C.), Greek historian of the wars between the Greeks and the Persians in 490 and 480/79 B.C.

4. See *Histories* 3.38. Pindar of Cynoscephalae in Boeotia (c.518–438 B.C.) was a lyric poet famous for his odes celebrating those who achieved victories in the Olympic and other games.

PLATO: You've shifted ground, Axiothea. Earlier you said that values were relative to the individual. Now you seem to be saying that they're relative to cultures or societies.

AXIOTHEA: Cultures, individuals—what difference does it make? Values are relative either way, not absolute as you claim.

PLATO: I think it may not, in the end, make a whole lot of difference—at least, not when cultures come into conflict over values. Then it will be just the way it is in the individual case. The only options will be a power struggle of some sort, since rational persuasion will be ruled out. Nonetheless, I think it's often the alleged fact of cultural differences about values that leads people to adopt some form of relativism.

Now, the first point I want to make about these differences is that they're only part of the story. After all, the reality is that some ethical values have weight in virtually every human community. These include obligations of members of a family to support their kin; obligations of reciprocity, to return favors done and gifts received; and constraints on sexual relationships. Cultural relativism can't explain why this should be so. Similarly, with Herodotus, he's very taken with differences, because these excite his curiosity and make for a good story. But he doesn't seem to notice the similarities that are at least as profound as the differences. For example, he's struck by the fact that the Greeks cremate their dead, while the Indians eat theirs, but not by the fact that both have funeral rituals and think the proper treatment of the dead to be a very important matter. So my first point, to reiterate, is that cultural relativists are overly impressed by differences and are unable to account for the equally startling similarities.

My second point is this. You said that Persian justice is different from Greek justice. How do you know that? Isn't it as follows? You hear the Persians using a word, X (I'm afraid I don't know any Persian words), and see them applying it in a variety of contexts in which you'd apply the word *just*. So you come to the conclusion that X is the Persian equivalent of our word *justice*. Then you notice that they also apply X to some things that we think not to be just. So you come to the conclusion that Persian justice differs from Greek justice. Isn't that right?

AXIOTHEA: Yes.

PLATO: Well, I'm not sure the argument is a good one. You see, what strikes me about it is this: if X weren't very close in meaning to 'justice', if it didn't mean pretty much the same thing, then it would be a mistake to translate it as 'justice'. If it is a mistake, we can't use the account to show that Persian justice is radically different from Greek justice. But if it isn't a mistake, and X really does mean the same as 'justice', Persian justice must be much the same as Greek justice—or very similar to it. And the same applies to all value terms, and all values.

AXIOTHEA: But, Plato, there must be something wrong with that argument. For it's just plain obvious that different cultures do have different conceptions of justice.

PLATO: What's obvious, I think, is that cultures differ about what things are just. Some think it's just for a man to kill his kin's killer; others think that's unjust and require the alleged murderer to be tried by a jury and to be punished by the state if he's found guilty. But that difference may be due to other factors besides a difference in what they think justice is. After all, we Athenians once held the former view and then came to hold the latter. And we didn't change our minds because we were forced to or because clever rhetoricians bamboozled us into doing so. No, indeed. We changed our minds for good reasons. We discovered that kin revenge was a bad way of ensuring that justice was done, and that jury trials were better. Remember Aeschylus' *Oresteia*, which deals with, among other things, that very issue? Similarly, we Athenians consider it just to prevent women from participating in politics, or from taking up various professions and occupations. Instead, we consider it right to sequester them in the household. But we're mistaken. And I think you agree that we are. Why? Because this way of treating women is based on false beliefs about women's natures and what women are capable of. You're a living proof of their falsity, since you're as good at geometry as any man here. But these beliefs are factual beliefs. In the end, the facts—not force or irrational persuasion—will prove them false, and then we will treat women differently.

AXIOTHEA: You make it sound so simple, Plato. You make it seem that the deep differences between cultures will be resolved once the facts, and the problems inherent in their various systems of values, are resolved. But you know it isn't like that. Even if there are absolute values, and we agree about them, we can never have absolutely certain knowledge of them. In this respect, too, ethics isn't like geometry. In geometry, there are truths we can grasp with complete confidence, and demonstrate rigorously to those who doubt them. But in ethics, even if there are absolute truths, we can't know them with certainty, and we certainly can't demonstrate them to doubters.

PLATO: Nonetheless, we do sometimes change our minds about values for good reason or because we recognize that some of our beliefs are false. I've shown that. I agree with you, however, that arguments in ethics are seldom like arguments in geometry. But I probably disagree with you about why that's so. You see, I think it's extremely difficult to get someone ignorant of geometry or logic to follow a proof or a technical argument. Usually, you have to provide him with a lot of specialized education before he even knows what the various terms in a proof actually mean and why it is that one thing follows from another. The same is obviously true in all the other sciences. If people had as much education in ethics as our students do in geometry, maybe we could provide them with proofs that are as hard and fast as geometrical ones. On the other hand, just as with geometry, not everyone is going to be capable of such education. So, even if it were a lot more widespread than it is now, there'd still be people who'd have to take their ethics—like their geometry or their medicine—on trust.

AXIOTHEA: You really think that if people were educated in ethics, as they are in geometry, ethical disputes, at least among the educated, would be like geometrical proofs? That just seems crazy to me. I mean, we already have an extraordinarily developed geometry. We know that geometry's a science. But ethics, Plato—what do we have in the way of ethics? Socrates looked high and low for someone with scientific knowledge of ethics, and he didn't find anyone. So he concluded that a science of ethics, if it existed, was something only a god could possess, and that human beings have to make do with something a lot more modest. Their wisdom, he claimed, amounts to nothing more than their recognition that when it comes to justice, temperance, courage, and the other most important things, they know only that they know nothing.[5]

---

5. See *Apology* 20e–23b.

PLATO: I see you've been reading my early dialogues, Axiothea! So let me tell you that I initially agreed with Socrates. I thought ethics was a science for gods, not mortals. But that was before I discovered mathematics. For mathematics brings absolutely certain knowledge to areas that had previously seemed just as muddled and undeveloped as ethics does now. Consider musical harmony and the movements of the planets. Before we had mathematical accounts of them, what we had by way of knowledge was scarcely worth mentioning. People used to argue endlessly, without any consensus emerging. Now that we understand these matters clearly, agreement is nearly universal. I see no reason to believe that human values will prove to be any different, once we get an adequate mathematical theory of them.

AXIOTHEA: So you're saying that Socrates was pessimistic because he knew no science? Are you, then, optimistic because you do?

PLATO: No, just realistic. I think ethics is a very young science, which has been practiced by very few first-rate minds. Why, Socrates was pretty much the first to devote himself entirely to it. Moreover, in many cultures ethics is bound up with religion, and that makes clear, rational scrutiny of it difficult. The fate of Socrates is testimony to that. Just because he questioned people about values, he was prosecuted for impiety. And that happened in Athens, the freest and most tolerant and most democratic city in Greece. Imagine what his fate would have been in Phlius, if what you tell me about it is correct! So religion is one obstacle to the development of a scientific ethics. But it isn't the only one. You see, ethics is also bound up with political power, and that, too, is an obstacle to clear, objective thought about it. Remember what Thrasymachus says in *Republic* 1?

AXIOTHEA: He says justice is the interest or advantage of the stronger (339a).

PLATO: Indeed, he does. And he isn't wrong in what he says, even if he doesn't quite see what its consequences are. After all, our values *do* reflect the power structure of our society. And the values instilled in us as young children do, in fact, serve the interests not necessarily of ourselves, but of those with the power to shape societal norms to suit themselves. You know full well that even here in Athens the laws embody the interests not of everyone in the city, but of the poorest classes, because our democratic constitution puts political power in the hands of the greatest numbers. So the actual distribution of power in societies is another reason why a scientific ethics has not emerged: clear thought about values simply wouldn't serve the interests of those in power. Fortunately, culture's hold over us isn't absolute. If we're lucky, we can gain a critical perspective on our culture's values and show where they're mistaken or inadequate. I was able to do that to some extent in the *Republic*, thanks to Socrates and the mathematics I learned from the Pythagoreans.[6] In part because of reading it, your mother helped to set you free. For, as you said yourself, if I hadn't persuaded her that it's just for women to receive the same education and have the same social roles as men of equal ability, you wouldn't be here!

AXIOTHEA: True enough, Plato. But if I'd been sent to the kallipolis you describe in the *Republic*, instead of to Athens and the Academy, I'd have been worse off than in Phlius, not better off. For, as I said at the beginning, what's wonderful about my life here is that I'm free to be and do what I want. Whereas in the kallipolis, I'd be a breeding machine for society, forced to have sex with pimply young men and watch wrinkled old ones exercising naked in the gym.

PLATO: Indeed, you did say that at the beginning. But, as I remember, you quickly changed your mind. For you, too, admitted that it would be bad if people were free to satisfy all their desires, since some of those desires are bad, while others, if they were satisfied, would quickly take away the freedom to satisfy others.

AXIOTHEA: True. But I also said that *I* wanted to be the one to decide which of my desires I should satisfy, because freedom and self-determination are so much more important than other values.

PLATO: Do you mean *really* more important? Or just more important *to you*?

AXIOTHEA: Oh, Plato, I see problems either way! But since I want an argument and not just to be overpowered or seduced by a clever rhetorician, I know I'd better say that freedom and self-determination are really more important. It isn't just my view, or true for me, that this is so; it's *really* true, true for anyone.

6. Followers of Pythagoras of Samos (mid-sixth century B.C.), the famous mathematician and philosopher.

PLATO: In exercising your freedom and self-determination, Axiothea, do you want to do so wisely, when you're thinking clearly and are fully aware of all the relevant facts? Or do you think that foolish and ignorant self-determination is just as valuable as the wise and knowledgeable kind?

AXIOTHEA: Clearly, it's better to be wise and knowledgeable than foolish and ignorant.

PLATO: I should think so. But suppose that you aren't knowledgeable yourself, though you know someone else who is. Should you listen to your own foolishness or to his wisdom?

AXIOTHEA: To his wisdom, I suppose.

PLATO: And what he advises you to do, that's what you should do—even if, because of your ignorance, you don't fully understand why it's best?

AXIOTHEA: Yes. Though I think he should strain every nerve to help me understand as far as I can.

PLATO: Well, then, you must approve of the kallipolis! For it's a society where rule by those who are wise and knowledgeable results in everyone exercising self-determination not under the guidance of ignorance, but under the guidance of true wisdom or knowledge, whether his own (as in the case of the philosopher-kings) or that of someone else (as in the case of all the other citizens).

AXIOTHEA: You make it sound so wonderful, Plato, and yet when I look at the life I'd lead in the kallipolis, under the guidance of so-called wisdom and knowledge, I know it would be intolerable.

PLATO: Intolerable to you with your present desires, Axiothea, or intolerable to you with the desires you'd have if you'd been brought up in the kallipolis? For in the kallipolis, of course, you'd have the desires whose satisfaction amounts to stable, long-term happiness, whereas who knows where the desires you have now will lead. Perhaps in years to come you'll regret not having children, and you'll long for the social acceptance so seldom available to those who are cleverer or less conventional than others.

AXIOTHEA: If that does happen, I'll have only *myself* to blame. But at least I'll have had my own life, and not one mapped out for me by other people.

PLATO: Will you, indeed? Isn't it rather the case that now your life has been mapped out by a group of ignorant and foolish people, including your parents, your teachers, your democratic culture in Phlius, and your own, sometimes ignorant and foolish self?

AXIOTHEA: And you, too, Plato. Don't forget you! For if my mother hadn't read the *Republic*, we wouldn't even be having this conversation.

PLATO: I wasn't excluding myself, Axiothea. Maybe what seemed like my wisdom to your mother was just something that time and increased knowledge will also show to have been ignorance and foolishness.

AXIOTHEA: Wait a minute! Are you admitting that the *Republic* might be mistaken?

PLATO: Of course it might! I'm not a philosopher-king, you know! What I tried to do in the *Republic* was describe a society in which knowledge and wisdom, rather than military might or rhetorical skill, had the political power. I thought that a society like that would have to be best. But, in designing it, I used the most reliable information and arguments available to me when I wrote it. And even since then, I've grown skeptical about some of them.

AXIOTHEA: So in the *Republic* you were trying to imagine what things would look like when, at the end of a successful inquiry into values, we had a true and complete science of them?

PLATO: Yes, that's right.

AXIOTHEA: But how do you know what things will look like from there, when, as you have admitted, you're not there?

PLATO: I don't know. All I can do is try to describe how they will look, given what we know, or think we know, now.

AXIOTHEA: So, when we discover more about people and the world, we might find that the city described in the *Republic* isn't a kallipolis at all, but a kakopolis—a wretched city, not an ideal one?

PLATO: Yes, we might. But we'll find it out only if people devote themselves to the study of ethics as they now devote themselves to the study of natural science and mathematics. In a way, *that's* the major lesson of the *Republic*—that we must *search* for the good. If we assume, as you did when we began our conversation, that we already know the truth about values, and that the truth is that they're all relative, whether to a culture or an individual, then we'll be complacent where values (including the value of truth itself) are concerned. We won't even look for a science of values, since we'll believe that there's none to be had. What I've tried to show you is that such complacency is based not on facts or knowledge, but on half-truths and confusion.

AXIOTHEA: I'm not sure where that leaves *me*, Plato. I think I'm persuaded by what you say about relativism. I'm no longer so sure that there couldn't be a science of human values. I take your point about how religion and political power have posed an obstacle to the development of such a science, and that few geniuses have devoted themselves to its development. I even agree that absolute freedom would undermine itself, and that everything that looks like a growth in ethical knowledge is likely to impose some restrictions on desires that are now thought to be unproblematic. But I remain convinced of the enormous importance of self-determination and freedom. After all, how are we to investigate whether a science of ethics is possible unless we have the political freedom to do so? And how could we ever be certain enough that we had found such a science to give up the freedom to investigate further? That's what I don't see, Plato, and that's why I continue to feel troubled and somewhat repelled by the *Republic*. In the end, I'd rather have Attic pastries and Corinthian girlfriends than an absolute good that might prove to be just another tyrant in disguise.

A year or so later, Axiothea's father came to Athens and, over Plato's protest, removed her from the Academy. He had no other children and needed her to continue his lineage, so he wanted to marry her off to a rich, older man. Rather than submit, she swallowed hemlock, hoping to find her final freedom in rebellion and death. For a while, what she had done was the talk of Phlius. But before long she was forgotten, and her father's family, deprived of heirs, died out. In the Academy she was longer remembered. But time did its work there, too, until, finally, little was left of her besides her name, that of her city, and a dim recollection that she had worn men's clothes.

FURTHER READING

Richard Kraut (ed.), *The Cambridge Companion to Plato* (New York: Cambridge University Press, 1992) is the best general introduction to Plato. The same editor's *Plato's Republic: Critical Essays* (Lanham, Md.: Rowman and Littlefield, 1997) is a useful collection of classic papers. Themes and ideas touched on in these dialogues are further developed in my *Philosopher-Kings: The Argument of Plato's* Republic (Princeton: Princeton University Press, 1988). Some of the criticisms Aristotle gives of Plato in "Forms" are discussed in Gail Fine, *On Ideas: Aristotle's Criticism of Plato's Theory of Forms* (Oxford: Clarendon Press, 1993).